Here's Where

Here's Where

A Guide to

Illustrious St. Louis

Charlie Brennan
with Bridget Garwitz and Joe Lattal

Missouri Historical Society Press
St. Louis
distributed by University of Missouri Press

Library of Congress Cataloging-in-Publication Data

Brennan, Charlie, 1959-
  Here's where : a guide to illustrious St. Louis / Charlie Brennan ; with Bridget Garwitz and Joe Lattal.
       p. cm.
  Summary: "A guidebook to sites related to famous people in St. Louis, with anecdotes, interesting facts, and cross-references. Each entry is keyed to one of eleven maps of the St. Louis area"--Provided by publisher.
  Includes bibliographical references and index.
  ISBN-13: 978-1-883982-57-7 (pbk. : alk. paper)
  ISBN-10: 1-883982-57-X (pbk. : alk. paper)
  1. Saint Louis (Mo.)--Guidebooks. 2. Historic sites--Missouri--Saint Louis--Guidebooks. 3. Saint Louis (Mo.)--Biography--Miscellanea. 4. Celebrities--Homes and haunts--Missouri--Saint Louis--Guidebooks. I. Garwitz, Bridget. II. Lattal, Joe. III. Title.
F474.S23B74 2006
917.78'660444--dc22
                                2006024513

Distributed by University of Missouri Press
Printed and bound by Sheridan Books

Contents

vi   Foreword

viii   Preface/How to Use This Book

x   St. Louis City and County Map

1   Alphabetical Entries

144   Map A: Downtown

146   Map B: Midtown, Part 1

148   Map C: Midtown, Part 2

150   Map D: West Central City, Part 1

152   Map E: West Central City, Part 2

154   Map F: Clayton, University City

156   Map G: North City, The Ville

158   Map H: North County

159   Map I: Webster Groves, Affton

160   Map J: South City, Part 1

162   Map K: South City, Part 2

164   Entries by Subject

168   Sources

178   About the Authors/Acknowledgments

Foreword

St. Louis is not my birthplace nor my hometown. From the shores of Lake Superior in the Upper Peninsula of Michigan to the stunning desert of New Mexico and the rugged mountains of Montana, I have made a so-called home in many places. But my eighteen-plus years in St. Louis have taught me what "home" really is, how one can care so deeply for a place and become profoundly entangled in the past, present, and future of a particular piece of the planet.

My graduate and postgraduate education made me a professional historian. I was taught that my discipline was objective and that I could practice anywhere. In fact, it was a decided disadvantage for a professional to permit emotions and subjectivity to cloud practice. But now that I have put my own roots deep into St. Louis, I have crossed that line. More precisely, I have erased it. I am no longer objective about my place because it is home. Now I think that one must care about a place as a prerequisite for having a home, for belonging somewhere. My work is now an expression of my commitment to my place, and my place—my home—is St. Louis.

We are fortunate to be in an old city. Precious memories are attached everywhere, and not just those memories that we as individuals have constructed. The memories of the generations before us are still here, still operating on the streets where we walk, in the chrysanthemums that so gloriously decorate our autumns, in the pungent aromas of hops from the brewery and barbecue from outdoor pits in the summer. The very curve of the Arch and the much older arc of the Old Courthouse dome, the facade of the venerable Sumner High School and the remaining bluffs on the river down in Carondelet, all of these things tell us that we are not the first to inhabit this place nor will we be the last. We are just the living links in this story, and it is our obligation and our pleasure to keep the story going.

I don't know if Charlie Brennan thought all this out as he planned and prepared *Here's Where: A Guide to Illustrious St. Louis*, but one look at his manuscript told me that this book is a solid contribution to the story we are all forming of this place. Many of the sites featured here have been obliterated or changed beyond easy recognition—all the more essential that we have some sort of remembrance of the way they were, the part of our story they should occupy. Brennan is more than a history buff, a journalist, a radio and television personality. He is a preservationist, and, what I consider high praise indeed, a St. Louisan dedicated to his place.

—Robert R. Archibald, Ph.D.
President, Missouri Historical Society

Preface

Here's Where has several goals.

First, it connects people to dots on the St. Louis map. We know our area was once frequented by the likes of Mark Twain, Kevin Kline, Tennessee Williams, and Tina Turner. But where exactly in St. Louis (the book is limited to the Missouri side of the river) did these people live and work? We aim to answer that question.

In addition, many famous figures had unusual connections to our city. With this book, we learn about John F. Kennedy's business deal in a restroom, Ronald Reagan's stint in a broadcast booth, Tiger Woods's stop at a gas station, and more.

But we also learn both that St. Louis had a profound effect on great figures, T. S. Eliot and Arthur Ashe among them, and that St. Louisans had profound effects on America, with Susan Blow, Tom Dooley, Dred Scott, and others in this category.

Lastly, and for me the most fun, are the unexpected connections. Harold Ramis and Vincent Price lived on the same street. Bob Costas and Sheryl Crow lived in the same apartment complex. Clark Clifford and William McChesney Martin Jr. were high school doubles partners. Robert E. Lee paid rent to William Clark. Earl Weaver worked for the City of St. Louis, and so did Cool Papa Bell. Three Supreme Court justices lived here. Who knew?

I bet you know of a connection between a famous person/event and St. Louis. If so, please let me know at cwbrennan@cbs.com.

—Charlie Brennan

How to use this book:

Here's Where is arranged alphabetically. You can find your favorite people or places by flipping through the book—each chapter represents a letter of the alphabet. Alternatively, you can search by category—film, politics, sports, and so on—in the Entries by Subject at the end of the book. Some entries also have cross-references to lead you to related entries.

A map of St. Louis City and County is included in the beginning of the book. Eleven other maps focus on different regions, each coded by a letter (A–K). Each entry in the book is plotted on one of the eleven maps (maps are not to scale). To find your entry on a map, look at the exclamation point next to the entry. There will be a letter denoting the map it's on. There will also be a number in the exclamation point, which represents the place marker on the map. For example, Chic Young is coded as K11. Go to map K and find marker number 11, and you'll see the location of his home.

Exclamation points and map markers that are purple let you know that the site is still in existence. Conversely, white exclamation points and markers signify sites that no longer exist or have changed in use.

St. Louis City and County

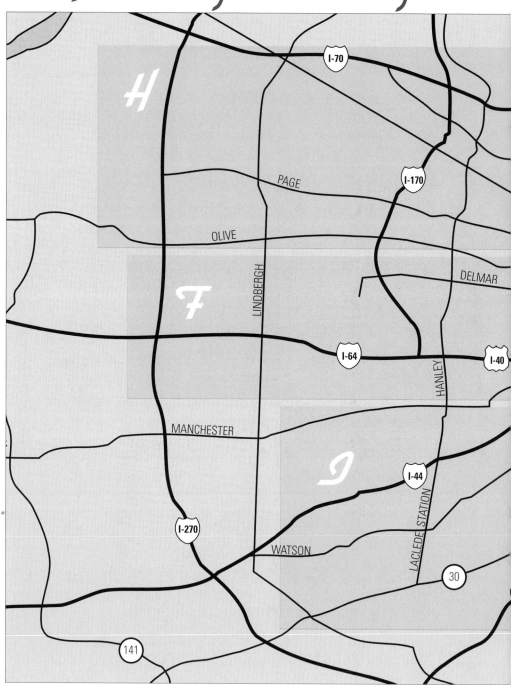

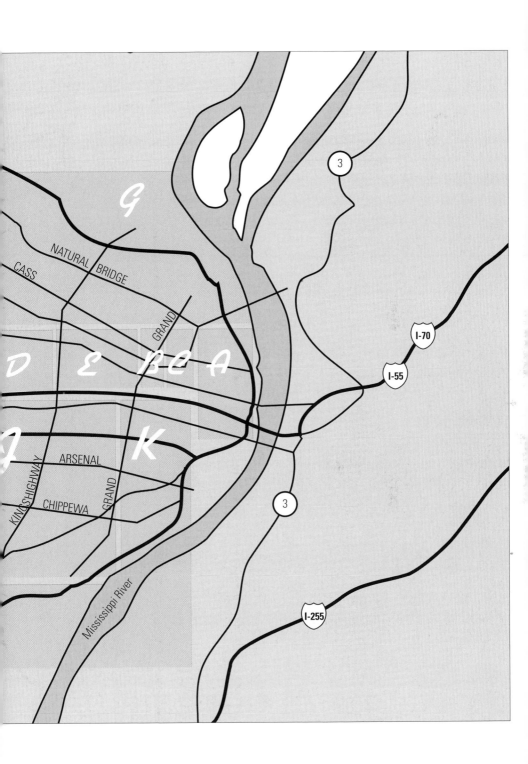

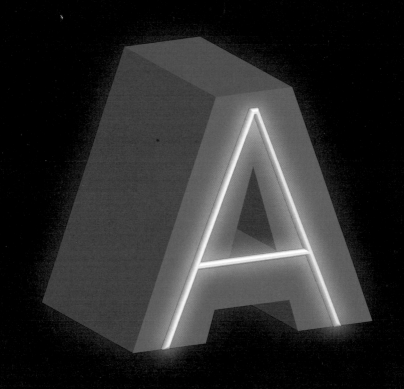

Aaron, Hank - Ashe, Arthur

Aaron, Hank

★ Sportsman's Park, 2901 N. Grand Avenue

One of baseball's greatest records started here: Hank Aaron belted his very first major league home run at the old Sportsman's Park at Grand and Dodier off Cardinal pitcher Vic Raschi on April 23, 1954. Over the next twenty-three years Aaron would hammer another 754 homers to become baseball's all-time home run king.

Sportsman's Park was demolished in 1966. The Herbert Hoover Boys Club now occupies the site. A baseball diamond is situated where the old one used to be.

American Legion

★ Old Shubert Theatre, 321 N. Tucker Boulevard

A two-month-old group of veterans officially adopted its new name, the American Legion, during a meeting at the Shubert Theatre, 321 N. Tucker Boulevard, May 8–10, 1919. Also at that meeting it adopted the preamble to its constitution, which begins, "For God and Country, we associate ourselves together. . . ." Today, the preamble is still recited at official gatherings of the American Legion in more than 15,000 American Legion posts worldwide.

Angelou, Maya

★ 3130 Hickory Street

Actress, writer, and civil rights activist Maya Angelou was born at 3130 Hickory Street on April 4, 1928. The author of *I Know Why the Caged Bird Sings* read her poem "On the Pulse of Morning" at President Bill Clinton's inauguration in 1993 and received an Emmy nomination for her 1977 perform-ance in *Roots*, the most-watched television show or miniseries to that point.

Angelou cont'd

* 2714 1/2 Caroline Street

Writer Maya Angelou was eight when she moved into her grandparents' home at 2714 ½ Caroline Street in 1936. In her autobiography, *I Know Why the Caged Bird Sings,* she described her neighborhood: "The Negro section of St. Louis in the mid-thirties had all the finesse of a gold-rush town. Prohibition, gambling and their related vocations were so obviously practiced that it was hard for me to believe they were against the law."

Armstrong, Henry

* 4145 W. Belle Place

Henry Armstrong, the only boxer to hold three championship titles simultaneously, trained at the old Slaughter Athletic Club, 4145 W. Belle Place. Armstrong held titles in featherweight, lightweight, and welterweight divisions from 1936 to 1938.

He also set a record for the longest series of knockouts.

The site on W. Belle Place no longer exists, though the club moved to Sarah Street in 1940.

* 2912 St. Louis Avenue

Boxing great Henry Armstrong served as associate minister at the Mount Olive Baptist Church, 2912 St. Louis Avenue, after he retired from boxing in 1945.

Ashe, Arthur

* 138th Infantry Armory, 3676 Market Street

Arthur Ashe, the first and only black male to win singles titles at the U.S. Open (1968) and Wimbledon (1975), practiced at 138th Infantry Armory, 3676 Market Street. Two months after moving to St. Louis in 1960 he won his first national title, the National Junior Indoor, at the Armory.

"St. Louis is one of the sine qua nons in my life," Ashe told the *St. Louis Post-Dispatch* in 1982. "If I hadn't gone to St. Louis, I wouldn't be where I am today. It was the first time I was able to play indoors. There were no indoor courts in Richmond [Virginia], and if there were, I wouldn't have been able to use them. I came to St. Louis for basically two reasons— Richmond was segregated, and at that time St. Louis had more quality players than any city outside greater Los Angeles."

Ashe died of AIDS at the age of forty-nine. The United States Tennis Association immortalized Ashe by naming center court at the USTA National Tennis Center, the main court for the U.S. Open, Arthur Ashe Stadium.

* 1221 Laclede Station Road

Tennis legend Arthur Ashe lived with Richard Hudlin at 1221 Laclede Station Road in Richmond Heights while attending Sumner High School in 1960 and 1961. He played tennis in the side yard.

Baker, Josephine -
Burroughs, William S.

Baker, Josephine

★ Gratiot Street, near Johnson Street (formerly Targee Street)

One of France's most beloved entertainers was born in 1906 in the Mill Creek Valley area of St. Louis near Union Station. Josephine Baker lived on Gratiot Street near Targee.

★ Union Station, 1820 Market Street; Soulard Market, 7th and Lafayette Streets

Growing up poor, entertainer Josephine Baker often searched for coal behind Union Station and for food behind the Soulard Market. She left St. Louis around 1919 and became the toast of Paris in the 1920s as an exotic dancer in *Les Folies Bergère* at the Moulin Rouge. She continued to perform on stage and screen in the 1930s and became a member of the French Resistance in the 1940s.

Josephine Baker.
Halftone, 1935. MHS Library.

Baker, Josephine cont'd

* Harris-Stowe State University (formerly Old Chauffeur's Club, 3133 Pine Street)

Entertainer Josephine Baker worked as a waitress at the Old Chauffeur's Club at the age of thirteen, around 1918.

* 2632 Bernard Street

Entertainer Josephine Baker lived at 2632 Bernard Street before leaving St. Louis in 1919.

Barkley, Alben

* St. John's United Methodist Church,
corner of Washington and Kingshighway Boulevards

Alben W. Barkley married Jane Hadley inside St. John's Methodist Church (now St. John's United Methodist Church) on November 18, 1949. The ceremony, which followed a four-month courtship between the seventy-one-year-old vice president of the United States and the thirty-eight-year-old widow from St. Louis, lasted nine minutes. It was big news: NBC-TV provided live coverage from outside the church.

The two had been introduced by mutual friend and St. Louisan Clark Clifford, White House counsel to President Harry S. Truman. In 1956, Barkley, then a U.S. senator from Kentucky, finished a speech in Virginia saying, "I would rather be a servant in the House of the Lord than sit in the seats of the mighty," when he clutched his head and fell down. He died of a heart attack as his wife watched from the front row. She died in 1964 of heart disease at the age of fifty-two.

See also Clifford, Clark.

Beaumont High School

* 3836 Natural Bridge Road

Beaumont High School's 1944 baseball team included five players who would go on to the major leagues: Earl Weaver (Orioles), Roy Sievers (Browns, Senators), Jim Goodwin (White Sox), Bob Wiesler (Yankees, Senators), and Bobby Hofman (Giants).

Bell, James "Cool Papa"

* James Cool Papa Bell Avenue (formerly Dickson Street between Jefferson and Webster Avenues)

One of the greatest early base runners and stealers lived on Dickson between Jefferson and Webster, now named James Cool Papa Bell Avenue, during his career with the Negro League team the St. Louis Stars. He played baseball from 1922 to 1950, before blacks were allowed to play in the major leagues.

Bell was the subject of many fantastic legends. He supposedly stole three bases on three consecutive pitches and scored from first on a sacrifice bunt.

Bell, James "Cool Papa" cont'd

His roommate Satchel Paige once said that Bell was so fast he could turn out the lights and be in bed before the room got dark.

Even though Cool Papa never had the opportunity to play in the major leagues, he was inducted into the Baseball Hall of Fame in 1974. He died in 1991.

James "Cool Papa" Bell as a Kansas City Monarch.
Photograph, ca. 1932. MHS Photographs and Prints.

★ City hall, southwest corner of Tucker Boulevard and Market Street

After retirement from baseball, James "Cool Papa" Bell, one of the greatest players in Negro League history, worked as a janitor and security guard in this building.

Benton, Thomas Hart

* Bloody Island in the Mississippi River, just north of the Eads Bridge near the Illinois side

To settle a feud, lawyers Thomas Hart Benton and Charles Lucas engaged in a duel at a distance of ten feet on Bloody Island in 1817. With the first shot, Benton struck Lucas in the chest; Lucas died twenty minutes later. Three years later, Missouri voters elected Benton to the U.S. Senate.

See also Grant, Ulysses S.

Thomas Hart Benton.
Photograph, ca. 1856.
MHS Photographs and Prints.

Berra, Yogi

J ! 5

⋆   5447 Elizabeth Avenue

When you reach a fork in the road, take it to the childhood home of Hall of Fame catcher Yogi Berra on the Hill at 5447 Elizabeth Avenue. Berra, born May 12, 1925, was a three-time MVP in a career that spanned nearly twenty years. The Yankee catcher was a member of fifteen all-star teams and played with the Yankees in fourteen World Series.

J ! 11

⋆   Wade Grammar School, 2030 S. Vandeventer Avenue

The Hall of Fame catcher attended Wade Grammar School in the 1930s. The building is now the site of the Meda P. Washington Educational Center, a school for pregnant girls.

J ! 10

⋆   Corner of Southwest Avenue and Kingshighway Boulevard

Yogi Berra sold newspapers on the corner of Southwest and Kingshighway in the 1930s. He wrote in his memoirs, "You don't have to be a financial expert to know the importance of money. . . . I learned that growing up on The Hill, a neighborhood of Italian immigrants in the southwestern part of St. Louis. My father worked in the brickyards and didn't have it too easy. He had a wife and five kids to support on a laborer's pay. Money for the things the family needed and the things us kids wanted was something you had to think about all the time."

Cardinals great Joe Medwick was one of Berra's regular customers. Medwick gave Berra a nickel every

time he bought a three-cent paper and told him to keep the change.

* Joe Fassi Sausage and Sandwich Factory, 2325 Sublette Avenue

Berra wrote in *When You Come to a Fork in the Road, Take It!*: "During the week, the factory whistle would blow at 4:30 in the afternoon—quitting time in the brickyard. That meant Pop would be home in fifteen minutes. And that meant I'd better get over to Fassi's, the corner tavern [Joe Fassi Sausage and Sandwich Factory at 2325 Sublette], and get a bucket of beer filled and rush home so it'd be on the table when Pop got there."

* Ruggeri's, 2300 Edwards Avenue

One of America's most humorous adages was coined at Ruggeri's restaurant sometime in the late 1940s or early 1950s. Baseball great Yogi Berra served as the headwaiter at this restaurant on the Hill during one off-season.

He later said, "Nobody goes there anymore, it's always too crowded."

The original Ruggeri's is now a banquet hall called Rose of the Hill.

* St. Ambrose Church, 5130 Wilson Avenue

From Yogi Berra's *When You Come to a Fork in the Road, Take It!*: "After working side by side in the brickyard, our fathers would play boccie in back of the Garagiolas' house. Our older brothers worked together as waiters. Joe [Garagiola] and I grew up and shared our dreams together. As kids, we played ball in the streets and sandlots, went to school and St. Ambrose Church, fetched our fathers' beer, and later worked in Sears Roebuck together; we were inseparable. Joe and I were even the best man at each other's wedding."

See also Garagiola, Joe.

Berry, Chuck

*   2520 Annie Malone Drive (formerly Goode Avenue)

The undeniably influential rock-and-roll guitarist Charles Edward Anderson, later known as Chuck Berry, was born at 2520 Goode Avenue, now Annie Malone Drive, in 1926. Berry became one of rock music's biggest contributors with such hits as "Johnny B. Goode," named after the street he lived on, "Sweet Little Sixteen," "Roll Over Beethoven," and "Maybellene." He was among the first inductees into the Rock and Roll Hall of Fame.

"Johnny B. Goode" was named after the street he lived on.

*   4420 Cottage Avenue

Berry's family moved to 4420 Cottage Avenue when he was six, in the early 1930s. The home still exists.

*   4319 Labadie Avenue

Berry's family moved to 4319 Labadie Avenue when he was seven, in the early 1930s. The home no longer exists.

*   4352 Delmar Boulevard

Chuck Berry's 1948 home, the first with his wife Themetta Suggs, was at 4352 Delmar Boulevard, in a boardinghouse owned by his uncle.

*   The Crank Club, 2742 N. Vandeventer Avenue

Around 1952, Chuck Berry used to play gigs at the Crank Club with old friend Tommy Stevens.

* Club Bandstand, 814 N. Grand Boulevard

Chuck Berry opened Club Bandstand in March 1958. He promoted bands and cabaret shows on the weekends.

Blackmun, Harry

* Missouri Athletic Club, 405 Washington Avenue

Harry Blackmun, the Supreme Court justice who wrote the landmark decision *Roe v. Wade*, was living at the Missouri Athletic Club when President Richard Nixon appointed him to the U.S. Supreme Court in 1970.

Blow, Susan

✶ 6303 Michigan Avenue

Susan Blow founded the first public kindergarten in the United States, at 6303 Michigan Avenue in 1873. The new concept spread from St. Louis to the rest of the nation.

Kindergarten classroom in the Des Peres School, established by Susan Blow.

Photograph by Emil Boehl, 1876. MHS Photographs and Prints.

Boston Red Sox

* Southeast corner of Pine and 4th Streets

This is the site of the Adam's Mark hotel, where the Boston Red Sox stayed in October 2004 when they "reversed the curse" of Babe Ruth by defeating the St. Louis Cardinals in the World Series.

* Busch Stadium, southwest corner of Broadway and Walnut Street

The 2004 Boston Red Sox defeated the St. Louis Cardinals to win the World Series at the old Busch Stadium. In the visitors' locker room, stains from the celebratory Mount Pleasant Brut Imperial champagne were still visible on the locker room ceiling when the stadium was demolished in 2005.

The site no longer exists; a new Busch Stadium was built just south of the old grounds.

Bowdern, Father William

* St. Francis Xavier Church, 3628 Lindell Boulevard

The movie and book *The Exorcist* are very loosely based on Father William Bowdern's experiences. Unlike his character in the movie, Father Bowdern survived the exorcism he performed on a young boy in 1949.

Father Bowdern kept mum about the incident for years after it occurred. When he wasn't driving demons away, he was the pastor of St. Francis Xavier Church on Lindell Boulevard.

See also Exorcism.

Bradley, Bill

* Missouri Athletic Club, 405 Washington Avenue

Future Olympic gold medalist, New York Knick, U.S. senator, and presidential candidate Bill Bradley practiced basketball on the fifth-floor court inside the Missouri Athletic Club in the late 1950s and early 1960s. He lived in nearby Crystal City and spent time in St. Louis while his father attended bank meetings, often on Saturdays.

Brandeis, Louis

* Old Courthouse, 11 N. 4th Street

Louis Brandeis, the first Jewish justice of the U.S. Supreme Court, was admitted to the bar inside the Old Courthouse.

* North side of Chestnut Street near Broadway

In 1878, Louis Brandeis had an office here facing Chestnut. He practiced law in St. Louis for about a year, then moved to Boston. He became the first Jewish justice on the U.S. Supreme Court.

Brock, Lou

* Dorchester Apartments, 665 S. Skinker Boulevard

Hall of Fame Cardinals base-stealer Lou Brock lived in this apartment building overlooking Forest Park in the 1990s, but he didn't steal anything here!

St. Louis Cardinals outfielder Lou Brock.
Photograph by Irving Williamson, 1969. MHS Photographs and Prints.

Brookings, Robert S.

★ Locust Street between 14th and 18th Streets (formerly 2329 Lucas Place)

Robert S. Brookings had a "bachelor residence" designed by Eames and Young at 2329 Lucas Place in 1888. This firm also designed Cupples Station, a series of approximately twenty warehouses, for Brookings and his business partner, Sam Cupples, which were located downtown.

Brookings is known primarily for moving Washington University to its current location and donating $200,000 for its administration building. He also founded the Brookings Institution think tank in Washington, D.C.

Brookings, Robert S. cont'd

* 5125 Lindell Boulevard

Philanthropist Robert S. Brookings moved here from his Lucas Place home in 1898.

* Washington University Alumni House, 6510 Wallace Drive (formerly Ellenwood Avenue)

In 1923, the new chancellor of Washington University, Herbert Hadley, remarked how much he admired the home of philanthropist Robert S. Brookings. "It is yours," Brookings replied before walking out with only his hat and coat. The next day he donated the house to the university as the permanent residence for the chancellor.

See also Compton, Arthur Holly.

Buchanan, Pat

* 8333 Delmar Boulevard

Pat Buchanan lived at 8333 Delmar while writing editorials for the *St. Louis Globe-Democrat* in the early 1960s. At age twenty-three, he was the youngest editorial writer for a major newspaper in the country. In 1966, Buchanan became the first full-time staffer in the legendary comeback of Richard Nixon and served as special assistant and confidant to the president through Nixon's final days of Watergate. He also served as the White House director of communications for Ronald Reagan.

Buchanan ran twice for the Republican nomination for president, winning the New Hampshire primary in 1996. He was an original panelist on three television news shows: NBC's *McLaughlin Group* and CNN's *Crossfire* and *Capital Gang.*

Buck, Jack

* 5405 Elizabeth Avenue

Jack Buck, Hall of Fame Cardinals broadcaster, lived at 5405 Elizabeth in the 1950s and early 1960s. Other famous residents of the street were Yogi Berra and Joe Garagiola.

* Charlie Gitto's, 207 N. 6th Street

In 1987, Cardinals broadcaster Jack Buck became the eleventh broadcaster to receive the Ford C. Frick Award, the most prestigious award in baseball broadcasting, presented by the National Baseball Hall of Fame.

"Mike Roarty [of Anheuser-Busch] and I were having lunch one day at Charlie Gitto's in downtown St. Louis. . . . I was told I had a telephone call in the offices upstairs. . . . It turned out to be Chub Feeney, the president of the National League. . . .

"'. . . You know why I'm calling,' Feeney said. 'You're going to receive the Ford Frick award.'

"'. . . The hair stood on the back of my neck."

Buck died in 2002. His son Joe followed in his father's broadcasting footsteps.

Buck, Joe

* 1 Memorial Drive

Broadcaster Joe Buck's career began on the seventh floor of this building at KHTR Radio, the FM sister station of KMOX Radio. Harry Caray and Jack Buck are among the legends who worked at this address.

See also Buck, Jack; Caray, Harry; Costas, Bob; Dierdorf, Dan; Philbin, Regis.

Bumbry, Grace

* 1703 Annie Malone Drive (formerly Goode Avenue)

Opera singer Grace Bumbry lived at 1703 Annie Malone Drive before attending Boston University and beginning her career. She appeared on the Arthur Godfrey television program *Talent Scouts* in 1954 and has performed at Carnegie Hall, the White House, London's Royal Opera House in Covent Garden, the Metropolitan Opera, and Milan's La Scala Theatre.

Grace Bumbry.
Photograph by Louis Melancon, ca. 1960s.
MHS Photographs and Prints.

Burroughs, William S.

* 4664 Pershing Avenue

The author of *Naked Lunch* lived at 4664 Pershing Avenue from 1914 to 1924 Later, he was arrested for the breaking and entering of homes in the Central West End.

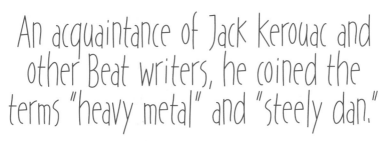

An acquaintance of Jack Kerouac and other Beat writers, he coined the terms "heavy metal" and "steely dan."

After spending most of his life addicted to heroin or alcohol, Burroughs died of a heart attack in Kansas in 1997 at eighty-three years of age. He was buried in an unmarked grave in Bellefontaine Cemetery in north St. Louis.

* 700 Price Road

Writer Willliam S. Burroughs and family moved to 700 Price Road in 1926.

* John Burroughs School, 755 S. Price Road

William Burroughs attended the John Burroughs School (no relation) in Ladue beginning in 1926.

* Taylor High School, 222 N. Central Avenue

William Burroughs graduated from Taylor High School in 1931. The site is now Taylor Park.

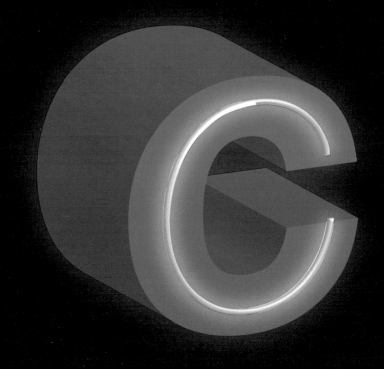

Capshaw, Kate - Crow, Sheryl

Capshaw, Kate

⋆ Hazelwood Central High School, 15875 New Halls Ferry Road

In high school, actress Kate Capshaw was already garnering attention for her acting skills. As a sophomore at Hazelwood Central High School, she accepted a Best Actress trophy at the 1970 Hazelwood Student Workshop Theatre Awards.

Working on a soap opera, she got her big break when she was cast as the female lead in the 1984 movie *Indiana Jones and the Temple of Doom.* She later married that film's director, Steven Spielberg, in 1991.

Caray, Harry

⋆ 1909 LaSalle Street

After Harry Caray's father abandoned the family and his mother died, he was raised by his aunt Doxie at 1909 LaSalle Street in the 1920s. He said of the area, "Compared to our neighborhood, the Hill (the tough Italian area nearby where Yogi Berra and Joe Garagiola grew up) was Beverly Hills."

Caray broadcast for the Cardinals from 1945 to 1969 and moved on to call games for the Oakland Athletics and Chicago White Sox, but most fans remember him for his broadcasts of the Chicago Cubs from 1982 until his death in 1998. Caray's large glasses, enthusiasm, and renditions of "Take Me Out to the Ballgame" during the seventh-inning stretch are now a part of baseball lore.

Caray, Harry cont'd

D 20

* Dewey School, 6746 Clayton Avenue

Harry Carabina, later known as Harry Caray, attended Dewey School at 6746 Clayton Avenue in the 1920s. He later recalled being teased at graduation when all the other boys wore white pants with their blue blazers and he could only afford plain gray ones. He said his "desire for personal success began on that never-to-be-forgotten day of humiliation."

K 4

* The corner of 18th Street and Chouteau Avenue

"My first job was selling newspapers in the afternoon. This is when I was eight, nine, ten years old. I started at the corner of Eighteenth and Chouteau, a wiry little kid selling the evening *Post-Dispatch* to the workers who were getting off the day shift at the International Shoe Factory. . . . I was always shouting those headlines. . . . Looking back on it now, I have to wonder if that isn't where I got my start in broadcasting."

D 19

* 825 S. Skinker Boulevard

"It was 825 South Skinker. I remember that to this day and will remember it as long as I live. The address changed my whole life." Harry Caray sent a letter seeking employment to KMOX Radio general manager Merle Jones, who lived at this address. Jones invited Caray to audition, then arranged for Caray's first radio job at WCLS in Joliet, Illinois. Later, Jones served as president of CBS Television from 1957 to 1968.

K 12

* The office of Edward J. Griesedieck, 1920 Shenandoah Avenue

In January 1945, Harry Caray convinced Edward J. Griesedieck to hire him as the play-by-play announcer for the Cardinals and the Browns on WIL Radio. Griesedieck agreed to pair him with Gabby Street over the objections of Griesedieck's own advertising executive, who thought Caray was too inexperienced. Caray went on to become one of the most famous base-ball announcers of all time and a member of the Hall of Fame in Cooperstown, New York.

★ In front of the Chase Park Plaza Hotel, 212 N. Kingshighway Boulevard

On November 3, 1968, while crossing Kingshighway on foot in heavy rain, Harry Caray was hit by a driver outside the Chase Park Plaza. Both of his legs, a shoulder, and his nose were broken. He spent the winter recovering in Cardinals owner Gussie Busch's beach house in St. Petersburg, Florida.

★ Towne Theatre bar, 210 N. 6th Street

After twenty-five years announcing Cardinals games, Harry Caray was hav-ing a few beers with his friend Tom Sullivan in the Towne Theatre bar in downtown St. Louis in October 1969 when he got a telephone call from the advertising manager of Busch Bavarian beer, Don Hamel. Hamel told Carey his contract would not be renewed. Caray later wrote, "So, after twenty-five years of never missing a game, of being the most loyal Cardinal sup-porter on the face of the earth, I got fired over the telephone in a saloon."

This site is now a parking garage with pedestrian-level restaurants.

★ Busch's Grove, 9160 Clayton Road

After being fired by Anheuser-Busch in 1969 from his announcing job with the St. Louis Cardinals, Harry Caray retreated from downtown St. Louis to Busch's Grove, a restaurant in Ladue. There he answered questions from TV reporters while holding a can of Schlitz beer.

The site's facade exists, but the interior has been entirely renovated.

Carroll, Mickey

★   8th and O'Fallon Streets

Four-foot, seven-inch Mickey Carroll was born here in 1919 before he landed a role as a Munchkin in the 1939 film classic *The Wizard of Oz*.

Cathedral Basilica

★   4431 Lindell Boulevard

The Cathedral of St. Louis became St. Louis Cathedral Basilica in 1997, after Pope John Paul II designated it a basilica. The basilica contains 83,000 square feet of mosaics—the largest mosaic collection in the world. The mosaics contain 41.5 million pieces of glass, known as tesserae, which were installed between 1912 and 1988—seventy-six years to complete!

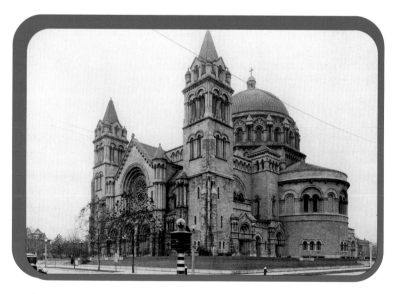

Cathedral Basilica, 4431 Lindell Boulevard.
Photograph by W. C. Persons, 1929. MHS Photographs and Prints.

Cedric the Entertainer

* 8422 Alder Avenue

Twelve-year-old Cedric Kyles and his family moved to 8422 Alder Avenue in Berkeley in 1976. According to his mother, Rosetta, Cedric often played football in the park behind their house.

In 1982, Cedric left home to attend Southeast Missouri State University in Cape Girardeau. After college, he lived in the St. Louis area working as a claims adjuster with State Farm Insurance. In 1991, at age twenty-six, he began his entertainment career by performing in comedy clubs.

Later known as Cedric the Entertainer, Kyles starred in movies such as *The Original Kings of Comedy*, *Barbershop* and *Barbershop 2*, *Intolerable Cruelty*, *Ice Age*, and *Madagascar*. He has also been seen by millions in commercials for Bud Light.

* Berkeley High School, 8710 Walter Avenue

Cedric Kyles, who is probably better known as comedian Cedric the Entertainer, graduated from Berkeley High School in 1982.

Charbonneau, Jean Baptiste

* Old Cathedral, 209 Walnut Street

Jean Baptiste Charbonneau, son of Lewis and Clark's American Indian aide Sacagawea, was baptized on this site in 1809. After spending the first several years of his life trekking across the continent on his mother's back, this young man was christened in a church where the Old Cathedral (Basilica of St. Louis, King of France) stands today.

Charbonneau, Jean Baptiste cont'd

Today, Charbonneau's face appears with his mother's on the gold dollar coin.

The Old Cathedral.
Photograph, ca. 1900. MHS Photographs and Prints.

Chirac, Jacques

★   Anheuser-Busch Brewery, 12th and Lynch Streets

If you dream of leading one of the most powerful countries in Europe, you may want to schedule an interview with Anheuser-Busch. In the 1950s the future president of France, Jacques Chirac, operated a forklift at this St. Louis brewery.

Anheuser-Busch Brewery brew house.
Photograph by W. C. Persons, ca. 1930. MHS Photographs and Prints.

Chopin, Kate

* 8th Street between Chouteau Avenue and Gratiot Street

Author Kate Chopin was born here in 1850. She went on to write *The Awakening*, *At Fault*, and *A Night in Acadie*. *The Awakening* is still among the most-read books on college campuses today. However, at the time of its release, the book created controversy. The novel's main character, Edna, experiences sexual desires beyond the confines of her own marriage, which represented a shocking departure for female literary characters of the day.

The house no longer exists, as Nestlé Purina is now located there.

Kate Chopin.
Retouched halftone, ca. 1899.
MHS Photographs and Prints.

* 1118 St. Ange Avenue

Ten years after her father's death in a railroad accident, Kate moved here with the rest of her family in 1865. Kate enrolled at the Academy of the Visitation the same year.

* 1125 St. Ange Avenue; 1122 St. Ange Avenue

Author Kate Chopin's husband, Oscar, died in 1882 while the couple and their children were living in New Orleans. Kate maintained his plantation for two years before moving to 1125 St. Ange Avenue in 1884 and then to 1122 St. Ange Avenue in 1885. This was the same street she had lived on more than fourteen years earlier.

* 3317 Delmar Boulevard (formerly Morgan Street)

In 1886, Kate Chopin moved to Morgan Street, where she wrote most of her novels and short stories, including *The Awakening*, *At Fault*, *Bayou Folk*, and her first literary publication, *If It Might Be*, a poem.

* 4232 McPherson Avenue

Kate Chopin moved to 4232 McPherson Avenue in 1903. In August 1904, she suffered a cerebral hemorrhage after a day at the St. Louis World's Fair. She died two days later at the age of fifty-four.

Clark, William

* Arch grounds (formerly on the corner of Main and Vine Streets)

Just north of the Gateway Arch, on the grounds of the Jefferson National Expansion Memorial, lies a triangle of land that millions of tourists pass each year while walking from their parked cars to the Arch. From 1816 to 1838 this was the home of explorer William Clark. Clark also owned a building on this property that served as a museum for his Indian artifacts. In the spring of 1838, Clark rented the empty museum building to Dr. William Beaumont, who needed a residence. At the same time, Clark rented a small cottage on his property to Robert E. Lee., a young army lieutenant. Thus, three preeminent historical figures lived together on the same property: Clark, explorer of the Pacific Northwest with Meriwether

Clark, William cont'd

Lewis; Beaumont, still recognized worldwide for his pioneering research of gastric physiology and the human digestive system; and Lee, commander of Confederate troops in the Civil War.

See also Lee, Robert E.

William Clark.
Oil on canvas by John Wesley Jarvis, 1810. MHS Museum Collections.

*   Southeast corner of Broadway and Olive Street

William Clark died in his son's home on the southeast corner of Broadway and Olive in 1838. He was most famous for exploring the Pacific Northwest with Meriwether Lewis more than thirty years earlier.

At the office building currently on this site, former U.S. Senator John Danforth spearheaded the government's investigation into the FBI's 1993 raid on the Branch Davidian complex near Waco, Texas.

See also Danforth, John.

Clifford, Clark

* 705 Olive Street

Clark Clifford, one of the most connected Washington "insiders" in the second half of the twentieth century, worked as a lawyer for the firm Holland, Lashly, and Donnell in room 700 of this building from 1928 to 1943.

Clifford later was White House counsel for President Harry S. Truman. He urged President Truman to recognize the State of Israel. Clifford defended John F. Kennedy over allegations his book *Profiles in Courage* was ghostwritten. He worked to downplay Ted Kennedy's expulsion from Harvard in 1951 for cheating. He told President Lyndon Johnson the Vietnam War was a losing battle. He was listed on President Nixon's enemies list.

He told the media that President Jimmy Carter believed the country suffered from "malaise."

He was the first to use the term "an amiable dunce" to describe President Ronald Reagan. Clifford died in 1998.

See also Barkley, Alben, and Soldan High School.

* 6633 Kingsbury Place

This was Clark Clifford's residence in 1930.

Clifford, Clark cont'd

* 4450 Westminster Place

St. Louis attorney Clark Clifford met Harry Truman for the first time at a cocktail party at the home of James K. Vardaman Jr., 4450 Westminster Place, in 1939. Clifford would later become Truman's White House counsel and confidant. Vardaman, the son of the governor of Mississippi, became a naval aide to President Truman and accompanied him to the Potsdam Conference; he lost his White House position in 1946. Truman's daughter Margaret later claimed Vardaman was kicked out of the White House when he developed a bad case of "Potomac fever." Vardaman told others Truman got rid of him because he wouldn't play cards or drink gin. The president did appoint Vardaman to the Federal Reserve Board in St. Louis in 1946, and Vardaman proceeded to vote against every Truman policy for the next seven years.

Compton, Arthur Holly

* Washington University Alumni House, 6510 Wallace Drive (formerly Ellenwood Avenue)

The 1927 Nobel Prize winner in physics and chancellor of Washington University (1945–1953) lived here. Compton chaired a committee under President Franklin Roosevelt to determine the feasibility of producing nuclear weapons. His research led to the nuclear reactors that produced the plutonium for the Nagasaki bomb in August 1945.

Compton is immortalized in a NASA observatory named after him.

See also Brookings, Robert S.

Connors, Jimmy

* 138th Infantry Armory, 3676 Market Street

B
10

The winner of eight Grand Slam singles titles and two Grand Slam doubles titles practiced at tennis courts here in the 1960s. Jimmy Connors won his first professional tournament in 1972 and held a number one ranking from 1974 to 1978. In 1975, he was upset at Wimbledon by another alumnus of the Armory's tennis courts, Arthur Ashe.

Costas, Bob

* Georgetown Apartments, 7880 Chatwell Drive

I
3

Broadcaster Bob Costas lived in the Georgetown Apartments while working for KMOX Radio in St. Louis in the mid-1970s. One of NBC Sports' most recognizable faces and voices, Costas has served as broadcast host for network Olympic coverage and has called the play-by-play during the World Series and NBA Finals.

* 1 Memorial Drive

A
42

Broadcaster Bob Costas is just one of many whose careers started at KMOX Radio. In 1974 he began announcing St. Louis Spirits basketball games there, and he spent the next seven years at the station.

See also Buck, Jack; Buck, Joe; Caray, Harry; Dierdorf, Dan; Philbin, Regis.

Crow, Sheryl

* Georgetown Apartments, 7880 Chatwell Drive

I
3

Singer Sheryl Crow graduated from the University of Missouri in 1984 and lived in St. Louis for two years while teaching at Kellison Elementary School on Hawkins Road in Fenton. She lived in an apartment at 7880 Chatwell Drive before she moved to Los Angeles in 1986.

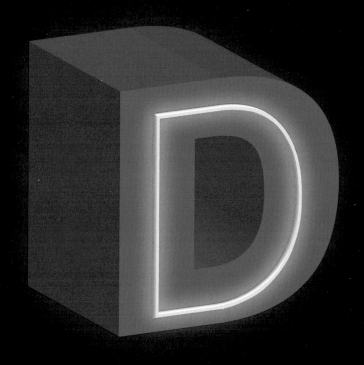

Danforth, John - Duvall, Robert

Danforth, John

* 17 Brentmoor Park

John Danforth, who served as U.S. senator as well as U.S. ambassador to the United Nations, grew up at 17 Brentmoor Park.

See also Clark, William.

Danforth, William H.

* 17 Kingsbury Boulevard

William H. Danforth, the founder of Ralston Purina, the maker of farm and pet feed known for its checkerboard logo, lived at 17 Kingsbury Boulevard until his death on December 24, 1955.

D'Arcy, William Cheever

* The Old Fullerton Building, Pine and 6th Streets

When William Cheever D'Arcy founded his St. Louis advertising agency here in 1906, he couldn't have known that D'Arcy would become one of the most celebrated ad agencies in the world. A young Atlanta company with a bubbly brown soda water was among the first to entrust its image to D'Arcy. In return, D'Arcy helped build Coca-Cola into the most recognized brand on the planet. *Advertising Age* magazine named "The Pause That Refreshes" the second finest ad campaign of the twentieth century. D'Arcy's work for Budweiser beer included the slogans "This Bud's for You" and "When You Say Bud, You've Said It All" and commercials featuring the Bud Bowl, the Budweiser frogs, and the famous Clydesdales.

D'Arcy, William Cheever cont'd

D'Arcy closed in 2002 after merging with another agency, and the Fullerton Building has been torn down.

See also Smith, Luther Ely.

Davis, Billy, Jr.

★ 3919 West Belle Place

Born in 1940, Billy Davis Jr. lived at 3919 West Belle Place while attending Cole School at 3935 Enright Avenue, going to the YMCA, and playing baseball. He attended Washington Tech on Franklin before joining the army.

After military service, he formed and sang in the Fifth Dimension, one of the top musical acts of the 1960s. The group's hits included "Aquarius/Let the Sunshine In," "Last Night (I Didn't Get to Sleep at All)," "One Less Bell to Answer," "Wedding Bell Blues," and "Up, Up and Away."

He and wife Marilyn McCoo formed a duo singing act with hits such as "You Don't Have to Be a Star (To Be in My Show)." They starred in their own 1977 television show on CBS—where budding comic Jay Leno appeared as a regular.

Davis, Dwight

★ 16 Portland Place

Dwight Davis lived at 16 Portland Place. Before serving as the U.S. secretary of war (now defense) in 1925, he was a champion tennis player who competed in the 1904 Olympics. In 1900 he donated a silver cup to an international tennis tournament and created the Davis Cup. (Another St. Louisan, George Herbert Walker, donated the trophy for the annual golf tournament that would bear his name, the Walker Cup). As parks commissioner for the City of St. Louis from 1911 to 1915, he built the first public tennis courts in the United States.

The house still has a red clay tennis court.

Dwight Davis.
Photograph by Arthur Proetz, ca. 1912. MHS Photographs and Prints.

Davis, Jefferson

*   Jefferson Barracks, 533 Grant Road

Jefferson Barracks military base has hosted many notable servicemen, including Confederate president Jefferson Davis.

See also Planter's Hotel.

Davis, Miles

*   Riviera Club, 4460 Delmar Boulevard

Jordan Chambers, the so-called father of black politics, ran the all-black Riviera Club, where Miles Davis performed with Billy Eckstine's band in 1944.

Dickens, Charles

*   Planter's Hotel, northwest corner of 4th and Pine Streets

English author Charles Dickens stayed at the Planter's Hotel during his visit to St. Louis in 1842 and commented on the city's weather: "No man ever admits the unhealthiness of the place he dwells in (unless he is going away from it), and I shall therefore, I have no doubt, be at issue with the inhabitants of St. Louis, in questioning the perfect salubrity of its climate, and in hinting that I think it must rather dispose to fever in the summer and autumnal seasons. Just adding that it is very hot, lies among great rivers, and has vast tracts of undrained swampy land around it, I leave the reader to form his own opinion."

The hotel closed in 1922.

See also Planter's Hotel.

Planter's Hotel.
Photograph by Emil Boehl, 1875. MHS Photographs and Prints.

Dierdorf, Dan

* 1 Memorial Drive

Dan Dierdorf played for the St. Louis (football) Cardinals from 1971 to 1983. He was named All-Pro six times and was inducted into the Pro Football Hall of Fame in 1996.

After retirement he became a sportscaster, beginning his career at KMOX Radio at 1 Memorial Drive. He has commentated on the NFL for ABC and CBS Sports and has been nominated for three Emmy Awards as Outstanding Sports Analyst, in 1987, 1988, and 1989.

Diller, Phyllis

*   Frederick Billings Chase House, 30 Mason Avenue

Big-haired comedienne Phyllis Diller lived here during the 1960s with her husband and five children. Her home life was far from amusing, as she wrote in *Like a Lampshade in a Whorehouse: My Life in Comedy*: "In the spring of 1962, I paid $20,000 cash for an eleven-room colonial house on Mason Avenue in affluent Webster Groves, just ten miles southwest of St. Louis—the children had lived there so long, it was their home, and this property realized my longtime promise to them that one day they'd each have their own room. It had a pink stucco exterior, white shutters, a pool in the backyard, and classic artwork and antique furniture throughout; yet with a husband and daughter both skidding off the rails, how could I enjoy any of this? Soon after we moved, I walked into [daughter] Sally's bedroom and discovered her sitting facing the corner with a razor blade in her hand. That's when I realized she had to go into an institution."

Dooley, Tom

*   6940 Pershing Avenue

Tom Dooley lived his first seven years at 6940 Pershing, from 1927 until 1934. Later, as a young Navy doctor, Dooley tended to thousands of North Vietnamese fleeing for the south. His book *Deliver Us from Evil* was condensed by *Reader's Digest* into fourteen languages.

*   6314 Waterman Boulevard

Tom Dooley moved here with his family in 1934 when he was seven years old. The family moved to Ladue in 1940.

According to polls, he was among the most admired men in the United States when he died of cancer in 1961.

Doolittle, General James H.

* 6311 Washington Avenue

General James H. "Jimmy" Doolittle (b. 1896) worked as a manager and pilot for Shell Oil in St. Louis while he lived at 6311 Washington from 1932 to 1938. He joined the war effort in World War II and led the first carrier-based bomber attack on mainland Japan in 1942. The fliers in his bombing missions off the USS *Hornet* became known as Doolittle's Raiders. He received the Medal of Honor from President Franklin Roosevelt.

Dreiser, Theodore

* 708 Pine Street

Novelist Theodore Dreiser lived in St. Louis from 1892 to 1894, working as a newspaper reporter. He later wrote the novel *Sister Carrie*.

Duvall, Robert

* The Principia Upper School, 13201 Clayton Road

Academy Award–winner Robert Duvall graduated from the Principia Upper School in 1949. He then majored in drama at Principia College in Elsah, Illinois, from where he graduated in 1953.

Duvall created the memorable character Lt. Col. Bill Gilgore in *Apocalypse Now* (1979), who delivered the oft-quoted line, "I love the smell of napalm in the morning." Four years later, he won the Academy Award for his performance in *Tender Mercies*.

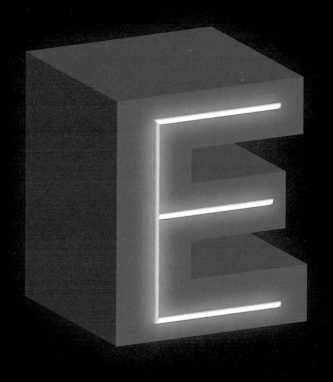

Eads, James B. - Exorcism

Eads, James B.

* N. Broadway and Clinton Street

James Buchanan Eads built the triple-arch Eads Bridge across the Mississippi from 1867 to 1874. He also designed ironclad boats for the Union during the Civil War. He lived at Broadway and Clinton early in his career.

James B. Eads.
Photograph by J. A. Scholten, ca. 1869.
MHS Photographs and Prints.

* Glassworks, 2300 N. Broadway

In 1845, bridge builder James Buchanan Eads's glassworks shop was located at 2300 N. Broadway, just down the street from his home. He was named after his second cousin, President James Buchanan.

Eagleton, Thomas F.

J
12

* 4608 Tower Grove Place

Thomas Eagleton, the U.S. senator responsible for the Clean Air and Water Acts, grew up in the 1930s in the house at 4608 Tower Grove Place. Eagleton also sponsored legislation to stop the American bombing in Cambodia, which subsequently ended America's involvement in the Vietnam War. He was a vice presidential candidate in 1972 and retired from the Senate in 1987. Eagleton later taught at Washington University and practiced law.

D
2

* 6168 Waterman Boulevard

Tom Eagleton and his wife, Barbara, moved to 6168 Waterman in 1956. They left for Jefferson City in 1961 after Mr. Eagleton was elected Missouri's attorney general in 1960.

F
27

* 268 Woodbourne Drive

Tom Eagleton represented Missouri as U.S. senator from 1968 to 1987. During this time the Eagletons lived at 268 Woodbourne Drive.

Edwards, Benjamin F.

D
11

* 10 Kingsbury Place

Benjamin F. Edwards, who founded A.G. Edwards brokerage firm with his father, Albert Gallatin, in 1887, built the house at 10 Kingsbury Place in 1905 to use as a residence.

Eisenhower, Dwight D.

* Jefferson Barracks, 533 Grant Road

Before he was the president of the United States, Dwight D. Eisenhower began his military career here, ten miles south of the Gateway Arch at Jefferson Barracks. A young Eisenhower trained here until 1911, when he left for West Point.

Eliot, T. S.

* 2635 Locust Street

Sometimes called the greatest poet and literary critic of the modern era, T. S. Eliot was born on September 26, 1888, in a house at 2635 Locust Street. He wrote such works as *The Waste Land*, *Four Quartets*, and *Ash*

Locust Street looking west to Beaumont.
The Eliot family residence is at 2635 Locust.
Photograph, ca. 1900. MHS Photographs and Prints.

Eliot, T. S. cont'd

Wednesday and won the Nobel Prize for Literature in 1948. His book of poems about cats, *Old Possum's Book of Practical Cats*, served as the basis for the the Broadway musical *CATS* by Andrew Lloyd Webber and may be Eliot's most popular and well-known cultural contribution.

The home no longer exists, but a plaque marks the spot.

* 1104 Olive Street

This spot has a connection to one of the most famous poems in modern English literature, T. S. Eliot's "The Love Song of J. Alfred Prufrock." William Prufrock owned a furniture store at 1104 Olive. Eliot used the store owner's last name for the main character of this poem.

* Smith Academy, 19th Street and Washington Avenue

Eliot attended Smith Academy, a prep school for Washington University, on the lower end of Washington Avenue from 1898 to 1905. He, of course, wrote the class poem.

The school closed in 1917.

* 4446 Westminster Place

T. S. Eliot's parents lived here from 1905 to 1919, while their son was studying at Milton Academy and Harvard. A plaque at this location celebrates the life of one of the most recognizable names in poetry.

* Eads Bridge

In a 1930 letter, Eliot wrote, "The river also made a deep impression on me; and it was a great treat to be taken down to the Eads bridge in flood time."

First Washington
University
Building and
Smith Academy.
Daguerrotype by Thomas M.
Easterly, 1856–1857. MHS
Photographs and Prints.

Escape from New York

* Old Chain of Rocks Bridge

In 1981 scenes from John Carpenter's *Escape from New York* were filmed on the Chain of Rocks Bridge. Here, the character played by actress Adrienne Barbeau met her untimely death. The action was supposed to take place in 1997 New York.

Exorcism

* Alexian Brothers Hospital, Broadway and Keokuk Street

In 1949 four St. Louis priests were involved with the infamous exorcism in the psychiatric ward at the Alexian Brothers Hospital at Broadway and Keokuk, which inspired the 1973 film *The Exorcist*. Legend says that construction workers discovered a diary hidden in a desk drawer before the building was destroyed and that the diary told the entire story about the exorcism, which the priests were not supposed to leak.

Alexian Brothers Hospital is now St. Alexius Hospital. It is still at approximately the same location, although the "exorcist building" is gone.

See also Bowdern, Father William.

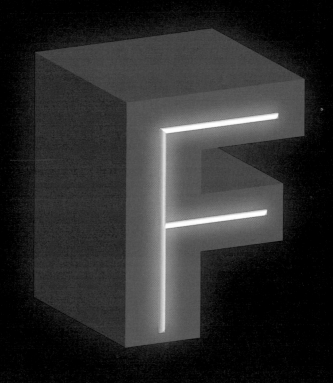

Field, Eugene -
French, Daniel Chester

Field, Eugene

* 634 S. Broadway

Eugene Field, the poet who wrote "Little Boy Blue," "The Duel" (The Gingham Dog and the Calico Cat), and "Wynken, Blynken and Nod," was born in this house in 1850. After his mother died in 1856, he moved to Massachusetts to live with relatives.

This was also the home of Eugene's father, attorney Roswell Martin Field, who defended the slaves Dred and Harriet Scott when they sued for their freedom in 1853. The Scotts' case led to a national furor and was a major contributor to the outbreak of the Civil War.

In 1902, Mark Twain helped honor Eugene Field by unveiling a plaque which remains on the building to this day. It would be Twain's last appearance in St. Louis.

The house is now the Eugene Field House and St. Louis Toy Museum. It's the only extant period row house in this section of St. Louis.

David R. Francis with Mark Twain at the Eugene Field House for the unveiling of a commemorative tablet.
Photograph, 1902. MHS Photographs and Prints.

First gas station

* 412 S. Theresa Avenue

St. Louis was home to the world's first filling station in 1905 at 412 S. Theresa Avenue. The gas station is no longer there.

First monster truck

* Chandler's Construction, St. Louis Avenue and Paul Drive

Bob and Marilyn Chandler used a Ford F-250 4×4 and kept adding different parts to it at their workshop in Ferguson in 1974 to put together what would become world's first monster truck, Bigfoot. After several modifications to wheels, axles, and other parts, Bigfoot eventually had sixty-six-inch tires, the tires that now define a monster truck. By 1979 the monster truck was making show appearances, and in 1981 the truck drove on top of junk cars for the first time. The Chandlers and their company have made more than fifteen monster trucks, and the company (now relocated in Hazelwood) still works on 4×4 trucks and parts.

Fort San Carlos

* 4th and Walnut Streets

A Revolutionary War battle took place in what is now downtown St. Louis on May 26, 1780. About 1,200 British soldiers and Indian allies attacked the small village of St. Louis, where Spanish and French inhabitants controlled the Missouri River and provided aid to the rebels.

The villagers built a stone tower called Fort San Carlos where 4th and Walnut Streets intersect today. Here they repelled their attackers, despite being outnumbered four to one. British plans for controlling the Mississippi and adjacent lands were foiled.

Fort San Carlos.

Ink on paper by Clarence Hoblitzelle, 1897. MHS Museum Collections.

Foxx, Redd

* 4400 Enright Avenue

The star of NBC's television series *Sanford and Son* was born at 4400 Enright Avenue on December 9, 1922. He left for Milwaukee after his father abandoned the family when Foxx was four. He later starred in TV shows on NBC, ABC, and CBS.

* 2900 block of Bell Avenue

After briefly living in Milwaukee, comic Redd Foxx lived on the 2900 block of Bell Avenue in the late 1920s. In 1973, parts of Spring Avenue were renamed Redd Foxx Lane.

* Banneker School, 2840 Samuel Shepard Drive

After returning to St. Louis from Milwaukee, Foxx attended the Banneker School, 2840 Samuel Shepard Drive, around 1930. He was expelled for returning fire after a teacher launched a book at him. After the expulsion,

Foxx, Redd cont'd

Foxx moved with his mother to Chicago, where she worked as a house-keeper for the vice president of the Chicago White Sox.

Francis, David R.

*   4421 Maryland Avenue

David R. Francis, the president of the 1904 World's Fair and the only person elected both mayor of St. Louis and governor of Missouri, lived at 4421 Maryland Avenue. The residence was completed in 1895 and took up an entire city block.

On April 29, 1903, President Theodore Roosevelt and former president Grover Cleveland both spent the night in the Francis home before attending the Louisiana Purchase Exposition Dedication Day ceremony. Although they were members of different political parties, they got along just fine.

The home, last used by the Francis family for David's funeral in 1927, has been demolished.

David R. Francis.
Photograph by Toshiro Kajiwara, ca. 1910.
MHS Photographs and Prints.

★ Northwest corner of Pine and Fourth Streets

David R. Francis was president of the Mississippi Valley Trust Company, at the corner of Pine and Fourth, which provided financial backing for the St. Louis World's Fair in 1904. Francis was also president of the Fair.

The 1896 building is still standing.

Francis Field

★ Northeast corner of Big Bend and Forsyth Boulevards

A former Olympic Stadium sits the northeast corner of Big Bend and Forsyth Boulevards. The first Olympics in the United States was held in St. Louis in 1904. Since then, only Los Angeles and Atlanta have joined St. Louis as hosts of the Summer Games. Francis Field, named after Olympics and World's Fair organizer David R. Francis, is now home to athletes at Washington University.

"Frankie and Johnny"

C 19

* 212 Johnson (formerly Targee) Street between 14th and 15th Streets

The story behind the famous song began here with Frankie Baker, a nineteenth-century harlot who lived at 212 Targee Street. As the song goes, she met a man she called Johnny. He frequented with other women, and Frankie eventually shot her lover on October 15, 1899. She was acquitted in court, but the song about the incident followed her until her death in an Oregon mental institution in 1950.

Frann, Mary

* Nerinx Hall, 530 E. Lockwood Avenue

Known then as Mary Frances Luecke, actress Mary Frann attended and graduated from Nerinx Hall in 1961. She was named Junior Miss America that same year. After high school, she worked as a weather reporter for NBC's local affiliate.

Although she appeared in several television shows and movies, she is probably best remembered for playing Joanna Loudon, wife to Bob Newhart's Dick Loudon on the television sitcom *Newhart*, which ran from 1982 to 1990.

Frann died in her sleep September 23, 1998, of heart failure, in Beverly Hills, California.

French, Daniel Chester

★ Old Post Office, 815 Olive Street

The Old Post Office's architectural sculpture, *America at War and Peace*, was designed by Daniel Chester French. The original marble sculpture group has been restored and is now on the first floor inside the building; on the exterior is a molded replica. French is best known for his sculpture of Abraham Lincoln in the Lincoln Memorial in Washington, D.C. He also created the Concord Minuteman statue in Concord, Massachusetts, and the statue of John Harvard at Harvard University in Cambridge, Massachusetts.

This site has been renovated and now houses the Missouri Court of Appeals, Eastern District, and Webster University's downtown campus, among other tenants.

See also Mullett, A. B.

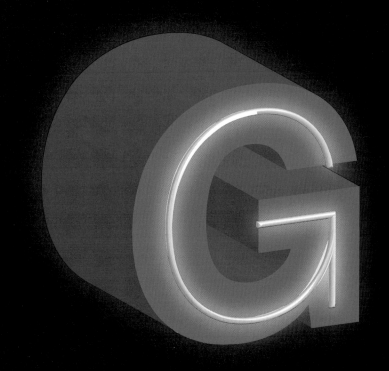

Gaedel, Eddie - Guillaume, Robert

Gaedel, Eddie

* Sportsman's Park, 2901 N. Grand Avenue

The most publicized stunt in baseball history took place August 19, 1951, at Sportsman's Park when three-foot, seven-inch, sixty-five-pound dwarf Eddie Gaedel emerged from a papier-mâché cake wearing the number ⅛ on his back to pinch hit for the St. Louis Browns. Gaedel was instructed to crouch low; his strike zone measured 1½ inches. Detroit pitcher Bob Cain walked Gaedel, throwing four straight balls.

To find a uniform to fit Gaedel, Browns owner Bill Veeck had to borrow one from the bat boy, Bill DeWitt. DeWitt later owned part of the Texas Rangers with future president George W. Bush and then led a group of investors to purchase the St. Louis Cardinals in 1995.

Sportsman's Park closed in 1966. The Herbert Hoover Boys Club is now located at the site.

Aerial view of Sportsman's Park.
Photograph by Ted McCrea, 1955. MHS Photographs and Prints.

Garagiola, Joe

J
7

*   5446 Elizabeth Avenue

Joe Garagiola grew up in the house at 5446 Elizabeth Avenue, next door to Yogi Berra and his family. Garagiola played in the major leagues for nine years, catching for the Cardinals, Pirates, Cubs, and Giants. His fifty-year broadcast career included work on St. Louis Cardinals and Arizona Diamondbacks play-by-play, the World Series, NBC's *Game of the Week*, and the *Today* show. Garagiola was inducted into the broadcasters' wing of the Baseball Hall of Fame in Cooperstown, New York, in 1991.

Elizabeth Avenue has been renamed Hall of Fame Drive in honor of three former residents in the Baseball Hall of Fame: Garagiola, Berra, and Jack Buck.

See also Berra, Yogi; Buck, Jack.

Gellhorn, Martha

E
21

*   4366 McPherson Avenue

Martha Gellhorn (1908–1998) lived on McPherson Avenue as a young girl. She went on to a sixty-year career as a war journalist, covering almost every major conflict from the Spanish Civil War to the communist takeover of China. She married Ernest Hemingway and was the only of his three wives to leave him. The London *Daily Telegraph* hailed Gellhorn as one of the greatest war correspondents of the twentieth century.

Gephardt, Richard

J
2

*   6263 Reber Place

Future congressional leader and presidential candidate Richard Gephardt lived with his family at 6263 Reber Place from 1941 to 1964.

* Mason School, 6031 Southwest Avenue

Richard Gephardt attended grade school at Mason School from 1946 to 1954. He returned to the school's gym in February 2003 to officially announce his candidacy for the 2004 presidential election.

* 705 Olive Street

Richard Gephardt started his law career inside this building in 1965, working for the firm Thompson and Mitchell. He was elected to Congress in 1976 and served through 2004. Gephardt led Capitol Hill Democrats as both majority leader and minority leader and ran for president in 1988 and 2004. The 705 Olive Street building was designed by famed Chicago architect Louis Sullivan.

Gibson, Bob

* 6316 Westminster Boulevard

During the summer of 1967, as the St. Louis Cardinals worked their way to the National League pennant and an eventual World Series victory over the Boston Red Sox, their ace pitcher and future Hall of Famer Bob Gibson lived in the house at 6316 Westminster Boulevard.

St. Louis Cardinals pitcher Bob Gibson.
Photograph, ca. 1960s. MHS Photographs and Prints.

Gilbert, Cass

D **15**

⋆ Saint Louis Art Museum, Forest Park, 1 Fine Arts Drive

Architect Cass Gilbert designed the Palace of Fine Arts (now the Saint Louis Art Museum) in the early twentieth century and later went on to build the U.S. Supreme Court Building.

The Saint Louis Art Museum is the only of the World's Fair "palaces" still standing and in use.

C **14**

⋆ St. Louis Public Library, 1301 Olive Street

The St. Louis Public Library was designed by Cass Gilbert. The library opened in 1912.

Glass Menagerie, The

D **16**

⋆ Forest Park

In Tennesee Williams's *The Glass Menagerie*, the character Laura spent too much time at the Saint Louis Art Museum, the Saint Louis Zoo's Bird House, and the Jewel Box in Forest Park instead of studying in school.

Goodman, John

★ Affton High School, 8309 Mackenzie Road

Actor John Goodman acted in school productions of *Li'l Abner* and *Hello, Dolly!* while a student at Affton High School in the late 1960s and 1970.

He later became a household name while starring as Dan Conner in the sitcom *Roseanne* from 1988 to 1997. In addition, he has had enjoyed much success in movies, such as *The Babe*, *The Big Lebowski*, and *O Brother Where Art Thou?*

Grable, Betty

★ 3858 Lafayette Avenue

The star of one of the most famous World War II posters was born at 3858 Lafayette Avenue on December 18, 1916. Betty Grable's family moved to the Forest Park Hotel in 1922.

Grable starred in more than forty films, including *Tin Pan Alley*, *Moon Over Miami*, and *Coney Island*. In 1943 she was reportedly the highest-paid woman in the United States.

Grant, Ulysses S.

* Grant's Farm, 10501 Gravois Road

The future president of the United States single-handedly built Hardscrabble Cabin at 10501 Gravois Road in 1855. The land had been sold to Grant's father-in-law by Nancy Lucas, whose husband, Charles, was killed in a duel by Thomas Hart Benton on Bloody Island. Grant lived in the log cabin with his wife, Julia Dent Grant. The home was moved to Webster Groves in 1890, then to Forest Park in 1903 for display in the World's Fair, before returning to its original property.

The cabin is on display at Grant's Farm.

See also Benton, Thomas Hart.

Ulysses S. Grant's cabin, Hardscrabble.
Photograph by Oscar Kuehn, 1912. MHS Photographs and Prints.

★ Jefferson Barracks, 533 Grant Road

After graduation from West Point in 1843, future U.S. president Ulysses S. Grant was assigned to service at Jefferson Barracks in St. Louis.

See also Twain, Mark.

★ Southwest corner of 4th and Cerre Streets

Julia Dent and Ulysses S. Grant were married here on August 22, 1848. Grant's father, Jesse, an abolitionist, refused to attend because Dent's family owned slaves.

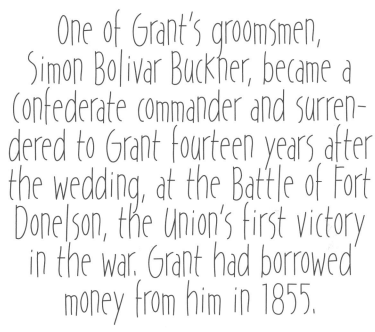

One of Grant's groomsmen, Simon Bolivar Buckner, became a Confederate commander and surrendered to Grant fourteen years after the wedding, at the Battle of Fort Donelson, the Union's first victory in the war. Grant had borrowed money from him in 1855.

Grant's best man, James "Old Pete" Longstreet, became a Confederate general. Perhaps that's why on April 9, 1865, at Appomattox Courthouse in Virginia, Grant wrote out magnanimous terms of surrender that would prevent treason trials. On that same day, while inspecting the Confederate lines, Grant met Longstreet and said, "Come on Pete, let's play another game of brag [a card game]."

Gregory, Dick

* 1803 N. Taylor Avenue

Civil rights and anti-war leader Dick Gregory was born at 1803 N. Taylor in 1932. Gregory ran for president in 1968 and devoted his life to racial equality. In 1992 he started the Campaign for Human Dignity to fight St. Louis neighborhood crime.

* Cote Brilliante Elementary School, 2616 Cora Avenue

Comic and political activist Dick Gregory said of his elementary school: "I changed a lot those years at Cote Brilliant [*sic*]. St. Louis had a segregated school system and that school had been built for white kids. But after the war, when the neighborhood changed, it became a Negro school. It had trees and lawns and a beautiful brick building. I had to walk through a nice neighborhood to get there from North Taylor. I stopped shining shoes that year because I wanted to go to school clean, without polish all over my hands. . . . In the three years that I went to Cote Brilliant [*sic*], I only missed school when I didn't have enough warm clothes."

* Municipal Theatre Association (the Muny), Forest Park

The Muny is the nation's oldest and largest outdoor theater. It was constructed in 1917. Dick Gregory went to the Muny as a kid, around 1945. He wrote in his autobiography, "But I guess the best thing we ever did was go to see the Muni [*sic*] Opera. Boo and I would walk and run half the day to get there, to sit up in the free seats for kids. *Carousel* and *Showboat* and *Roberta*, those were the kind of shows we'd see, the kind of music that really made you feel good. We'd sit up there and watch the conductors, so sophisticated in their tuxedos. We were so far away from the singers and dancers that we couldn't tell if they were white or colored. During the intermission we could walk down and watch the rich people smoke and talk and laugh. That was part of the show, too. Sometimes in the summer we'd go almost every night. It was almost like church. And then we could go home, and turn on the radio and hum along with the same kind of music we had heard at the Muni [sic], and close our eyes and the kitchen would disappear and we could see the whole show, all over again."

✶   Sumner High School, 4248 Cottage Avenue

Gregory wrote, "Then I went to Sumner High and I was nobody again. There were a lot of wealthy Negro kids at Sumner, doctors' sons who had their own cars. . . . The athletes and the rich boys and the brains were the big wheels at Sumner High School." However, Gregory set a state record in track while at Sumner.

Guggenheim, Charles

✶   329 Westgate Avenue

Oscar-winning movie director/producer/writer Charles Guggenheim, whose works include *Monument to the Dream* and *The Great St. Louis Bank Robbery*, lived at 329 Westgate from 1960 to 1967.

Guillaume, Robert

✶   1916 Lucas Avenue

Robert Guillaume was born here in 1927 and lived with his grandmother, Jeanette, without electricity or plumbing. He later portrayed the character Benson on the television show of the same name.

This site is now a parking lot.

Guillaume, Robert cont'd

* 15th Street and Washington Avenue,
  outside International Shoe Company

Future actor Robert Guillaume used to sell all three city newspapers on Washington at 15th in the 1930s. He also used to hide behind a billboard and blow spitballs at the Veiled Prophet as he came down Washington Avenue during the annual parade.

* 19th Street and Dr. Martin Luther King Drive (formerly Franklin Avenue)

The television and film star lived here during his teen years in the 1930s and early 1940s. Guillaume writes about his home in his autobiography: "We lived off a back alley in rooms that were dismal and dark." The site no longer exists.

* Geraldine Shoppe, Dr. Martin Luther King Drive
  between 19th and 20th Streets (formerly Franklin Avenue)

Around 1950, Guillaume opened a women's fashion shop called the Geraldine Shoppe on Franklin, in the same block as his home. The store was unsuccessful and closed within a couple of years, and is no longer there.

International Shoe Company, 1509 Washington Avenue.
Photograph by W. C. Persons, 1930–1932. MHS Photographs and Prints.

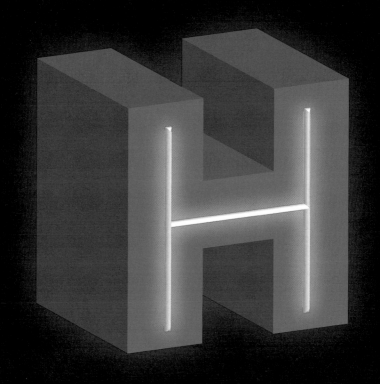

Handy, W. C. - Hurt, William

Handy, W. C.

* 14th Street and Clark Avenue (formerly Targee Street)

In the 1890s, a young W. C. Handy played music at 14th and Clark on what was then known as Targee Street. The city made an impression on him as he later said, "I've tried to forget that first sojourn in St. Louis but I wouldn't want to forget Targee Street as it was then. I don't think I'd want to forget the high-roller Stetson hats of the men or the diamonds the girls wore in their ears."

The Targee Street music scene peaked in 1904 and then sank into oblivion. But Handy wrote his biggest hit in 1914, "The St. Louis Blues," based on his experience in St. Louis.

By coincidence, eighty years later in 1994, the St. Louis Blues hockey team, named after Handy's song, would move into their new arena located exactly where Handy used to perform!

* Beneath the Eads Bridge

For two weeks in 1893, hungry and unshaven musician W. C. Handy slept on cobblestones under the Eads Bridge when he wasn't wandering the streets of St. Louis looking for work. He later recalled a woman along the levee who seemed in even worse shape. She cried that her man "had a

Handy, W. C. cont'd

heart like a rock cast in the sea." Those words became part of Handy's 1914 composition "The St. Louis Blues," which became one of the most recorded and performed songs of the twentieth century.

W. C. Handy (seated with cane)
visiting the Old Rock House Saloon in St. Louis.
Photograph, ca. 1935. MHS Photographs and Prints.

Hartford, John

★ 6940 Waterman Boulevard

Songwriter John Hartford grew up in the house at 6940 Waterman Boulevard. He wrote "Gentle on My Mind," which became a major hit for singer Glen Campbell in 1967. That same year the song won four Grammy Awards. Hartford died of cancer in 2001.

Heron, M. W.

★ 319 Pine Street

M. W. Heron, a bartender from New Orleans who later owned a bar at 319 Pine Street in St. Louis, invented the fruity bourbon Southern Comfort.

The liquor won a gold medal at the 1904 World's Fair.

Heron died April 17, 1920, three months after the beginning of Prohibition. He is buried in Calvary Cemetery in northwest St. Louis. Today his name is embossed on every bottle of Southern Comfort.

Hornsby, Rogers

A ! 4

* Jefferson Arms Hotel, 415 N. Tucker Boulevard

In 1926, Rogers Hornsby was a player and the manager of the St. Louis Cardinals when they won their first World Series by defeating Babe Ruth and the New York Yankees. In December, Cardinals owner Sam Breadon traded Hornsby, saying that if fans wanted to fight about it, they could find him having lunch at the Jefferson Arms Hotel.

The hotel is now an apartment building.

Hotchner, A. E.

E ! 4

* Westgate Apartments, No. 326, Delmar and Kingshighway Boulevards

The Westgate Apartments served as the setting for the Avalon Hotel in A. E. Hotchner's 1972 memoir, *King of the Hill.* During the Great Depression, Hotchner's family lived in the Westgate Apartments at the southwest corner of Delmar Boulevard and Kingshighway. Academy Award–winning director Steven Soderbergh turned the book into a movie. Incidentally, the residence was named the Empire Apartments in the movie version.

Hotchner also wrote the international bestseller *Papa Hemingway* and helped Paul Newman create his line of salad dressings.

See also Soldan High School.

Hurt, William

* Gateway Arch

The opening scene of *The Big Brass Ring*, featuring actor William Hurt, was filmed underneath the Gateway Arch in 1998. In one scene, Hurt, playing a politician running for office, answers reporters' questions (including one from *Here's Where* co-author Charlie Brennan). The script was based on the last unproduced screenplay by Orson Welles.

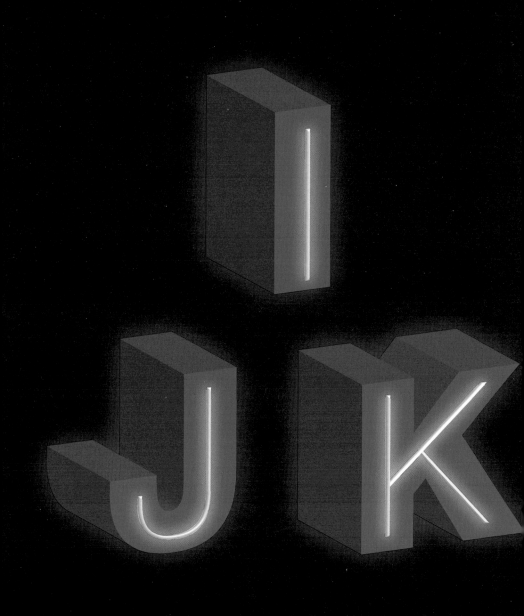

Inge, William - Kline, Kevin

Inge, William

★ Coronado Hotel, 3701 Lindell Boulevard

William Inge, winner of a Pulitzer Prize, an Academy Award, and numerous other awards, first lived at 3701 Lindell Boulevard when he moved to St. Louis in 1943. Inge worked as a drama critic for the *St. Louis Star-Times* and taught at Washington University. His interview of Tennessee Williams in 1944 led to an affair between the two.

He later wrote *Come Back, Little Sheba; Picnic;* and *Bus Stop* for the stage before they became movies starring actors such as Burt Lancaster, William Holden, Kim Novak, and Marilyn Monroe. He wrote and acted in the film *Splendor in the Grass*, which starred Natalie Wood and Warren Beatty. It earned him the Academy Award for best screenplay.

Alcoholism and depression burdened Inge, who sometimes could not make it to opening night of his own plays. He committed suicide in 1973, at age sixty, after receiving a rejection note from a New York publisher. His grave's headstone in Independence, Kansas, reads simply, "Playwright."

After serving as a residence hall for Saint Louis University students the building reopened in 2003 as a meeting and banquet center.

★ 1213 N. 7th Street (at Biddle Street)

Playwright William Inge lived at 1213 N. 7th Street about 1945.

★ 6168 McPherson Avenue

Playwright William Inge lived at 6168 McPherson Avenue around 1949, before he left St. Louis for New York.

Johnson, Philip

A
27

★ General American Life Building, 700 Market Street

Prominent architect Philip Johnson designed the slice-of-pie-shaped General American Life Building in 1977. A student of Frank Lloyd Wright, Johnson also designed the Seagram Building and the AT&T (now Sony) Building in New York and the Crystal Cathedral in Garden Grove, California, among others.

Joplin, Scott

C
3

★ 2658A Delmar Boulevard (formerly Morgan Street)

One of the most important ragtime composers lived in an apartment at 2658A Morgan Street at the time he created his 1902 composition "The Entertainer." Scott Joplin lived here from 1901 to 1903.

Much of Joplin's music enjoyed a rebirth when it was used in the 1973 movie *The Sting,* starring Robert Redford and Paul Newman. "The Entertainer" was a Top 40 hit in 1973.

The house is now a state historic site.

Scott Joplin House State Historic Site,
2658 Delmar Boulevard.
Photograph by David Schultz, 1993. MHS Photographs and Prints.

Kann, Stan

D 9

* 29 Washington Terrace

Stan Kann, who became known as the Gadget Comic on *The Tonight Show Starring Johnny Carson*, hosted a party for Carson in 1966 at his home at 29 Washington Terrace in the Central West End.

Kann appeared on *The Tonight Show* seventy-seven times.

Keckly, Elizabeth

A 12

* 5 Broadway (between Washington and Lucas Avenues)

Elizabeth Keckly lived at 5 Broadway until moving east in 1860. A former slave, she designed the inaugural gown for Mary Todd Lincoln in 1861. She became a confidante of Mrs. Lincoln, but the relationship ended in 1868 when Keckly wrote an inside account of life in the White House. She also worked for the wife of then-Senator Jefferson Davis.

Elizabeth Keckly.
Wood engraving, 1868.
MHS Photographs and Prints.

Kennedy, John F.

* Grant's Farm, 10501 Gravois Road

In 1960, Anheuser-Busch owner Augie Busch hosted a breakfast fund-raiser at Grant's Farm for U.S. senator John F. Kennedy, who was campaigning for president. Twenty-nine businessmen showed up and contributed $1,000 apiece.

Kennedy, Busch, and Congressman Tip O'Neill excused themselves from the breakfast and stepped into the men's restroom.

Busch had collected $17,000 in cash and $12,000 in checks. Kennedy took the cash and instructed Busch to give the checks to his assistant, Kenny O'Donnell. "That's how things were done in those days," O'Neill said. "When I first ran for Congress in 1952, I raised $52,000, and I don't recall seeing a single check. It was just the custom to give cash."

Kline, Kevin

* 7800 Davis Drive

In the late 1940s and early 1950s, actor Kevin Kline lived at 7800 Davis Drive. He later starred in such movies as *Sophie's Choice*, *The Big Chill*, and *Dave* and won an Oscar for Best Supporting Actor for *A Fish Called Wanda*. Kline has also won two Tony awards, for his roles in *On the Twentieth Century* and *The Pirates of Penzance*.

Another Broadway connection almost occurred near here: Tennessee Williams's father came close to buying a home in this neighborhood in 1936. Instead, the family moved into a rental home on Aberdeen Place, on the other side of Clayton.

See also Williams, Tennessee.

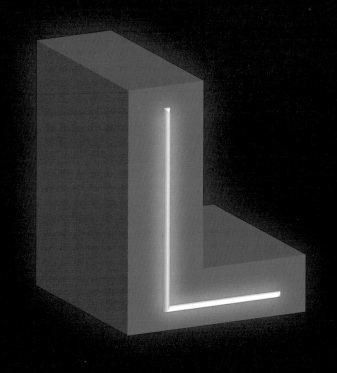

Lee, Robert E. - Lyon, Nathaniel

Lee, Robert E.

* Jefferson Barracks, 533 Grant Road

Many servicemen were stationed at Jefferson Barracks military base at some point in their careers, including General Robert E. Lee.

See also Clark, William.

Lewis, A. H.

* 6352 Forsyth Boulevard

A. H. Lewis, founder of the A. H. Lewis Medical Company, which began manufacturing the antacid TUMS in 1930, lived at 6352 Forsyth Boulevard.

Today the residence is home to the Catholic Student Center at Washington University.

See also TUMS Building.

Lindbergh, Charles

* 4th and Olive Streets

Harold Knight worked in the offices of Knight, Dysart and Gamble at the corner of 4th and Olive Streets. It was in that office that Knight and St. Louis Chamber of Commerce president Harold Bixby first met twenty-five-year-old Charles Lindbergh. Bixby and Knight agreed to give Lindbergh $15,000 for his upcoming attempt to fly a plane solo and nonstop from New York to Paris.

The site is now a parking garage.

Lindbergh, Charles cont'd

A 24 ⭐ Security Building, 319 N. 4th Street

Charles Lindbergh also visited Harold Bixby in the State National Bank inside the Security Building at 4th and Locust Streets in 1926. Lindbergh later flew over the building in his airplane.

Security Building, 319 N. 4th Street
Photograph by Emil Boehl, ca. 1906.
MHS Photographs and Prints.

E 8 ⭐ 1 Hortense Place

In 1926, Charles Lindbergh rang the doorbell of the residence at 1 Hortense Place and asked Earl Thompson for financial assistance for a solo nonstop flight across the Atlantic. Thompson would become one of Lindbergh's St. Louis backers. Another of Lindbergh's benefactors, Major Albert Bond Lambert, lived directly across the street.

A 5 ⭐ St. Louis Post-Dispatch building, 306 N. Tucker Boulevard

In his memoir, *The Spirit of St. Louis*, Charles Lindbergh recalled how a *St. Louis Post-Dispatch* editor rejected his pleas for financial assistance by telling him, "The *Post-Dispatch* wouldn't think of taking part in such a hazardous flight. To fly across the Atlantic Ocean with one pilot and a single-engine plane! We have our reputation to consider. We couldn't possibly be associated with such a venture."

Lindbergh did not name the editor who made these remarks. He does describe how he and his fellow visitor, Major Bill Robertson, reacted: "Major Robertson and I sit uncomfortably in front of the editor's desk. He hasn't even asked us any questions. There's nothing else to say. We get up, shake hands and leave."

Liston, Sonny

* 1006 O'Fallon Street

Future boxing champion Sonny Liston lived at 1006 O'Fallon Street with his mother in 1949, when he was about seventeen years old. He defeated defending champion Floyd Patterson for the heavyweight title in Chicago in 1962. He retired with a 50–4 record, including thirty-nine knockouts.

Dealing with crime and drugs his whole life, Liston was found dead in his Las Vegas apartment in 1970, reportedly from a drug overdose.

* Wedge Filling Station, O'Fallon Street and Broadway

Boxer Sonny Liston robbed the Wedge Filling Station on the corner of O'Fallon Street and Broadway of about thirty-three dollars on January 13, 1950.

* Unique Café, 1502 Market Street

Boxer Sonny Liston and several cohorts held up the Unique Café on January 14, 1950. The take was about thirty-seven dollars.

* 901 O'Fallon Street

Eighteen-year-old Sonny Liston drank at a bar at 901 O'Fallon Street, using the money gained from robbing area businesses in the winter of 1950. He would end up in the Missouri State Penitentiary in Jefferson City before the end of that year. By 1962 he would be boxing's heavyweight champion.

Liston, Sonny cont'd

* YMCA, Pine Street and Ewing Avenue

Future boxing champion Sonny Liston was released from the Missouri State Penitentiary on October 30, 1952, and moved into the YMCA at Pine Street and Ewing Avenue. The Pine Street Y was demolished as part of the Mill Creek Valley Rehabilitation Project in 1960.

* Tony's Gym, 4525 Olive Street

In 1953, future heavyweight boxing champion Sonny Liston trained at Tony's Gym.

* 4454 St. Louis Avenue

On May 5, 1956, boxer Sonny Liston was arrested at his home at 4454 St. Louis Avenue for assaulting a police officer. He was later sentenced to nine months in the city workhouse. Liston was arrested fourteen times between 1953 and 1958.

* 4439 Farlin Avenue

Sonny Liston's last residence in St. Louis was a house at 4439 Farlin Avenue. He shared this house with his wife, Geraldine, about 1957.

Lyon, Nathaniel

* Camp Jackson (also known as Lindell's Grove), bordered on north and south by Olive Street and Laclede Avenue, and on the east and west by Ewing Avenue and Grand Boulevard

A cross-dresser in Civil War St. Louis! General Nathaniel Lyon, a Union commander loyal to President Lincoln, suspected the state-controlled militia was secretly amassing munitions and preparing for hostile action against the United States. To inspect Camp Jackson, also known as Lindell's Grove, Lyon dressed as a woman and toured the area on May 9, 1861. Undetected with this disguise, Lyon departed the camp convinced federal forces needed to take military action. The next day, he moved forces to break up the state militia at Camp Jackson. Many St. Louisans, loyal to the state militia, rioted as a result.

The area is now the Frost Campus of Saint Louis University, named after Brigadier General Daniel M. Frost, leader of the state militia at Camp Jackson.

Camp Jackson.
Lithograph by Ch. Robyn and Company after George G. Friedlein, 1861.
MHS Photographs and Prints.

Martin, William McChesney,
Jr. and Sr. - Musial, Stan

Martin, William McChesney, Jr. and Sr.

* Northwest corner of 4th and Locust Streets

Prominent St. Louis banker William McChesney Martin Sr. helped President Woodrow Wilson draft the 1913 Federal Reserve Act creating the nation's central bank. Martin then became first president of the Federal Reserve Bank of St. Louis in 1929.

His son, William McChesney Martin Jr., started his career as a bank examiner in the Reserve Bank building at 4th and Locust Streets. He left St. Louis at age thirty-one to become the first paid president of the New York Stock Exchange. Although earning $48,000 per year, he left the stock exchange in 1941 to serve in World War II for $21 a month.

He later became chairman of the Federal Reserve Board, a position he held for nineteen years, serving Presidents Truman through Nixon. He said the role of "the Fed" was "to take away the punch bowl just when the party gets going."

See also Soldan High School.

Mason, Marsha

* Nerinx Hall, 530 E. Lockwood Avenue

Academy Award–nominated actress Marsha Mason graduated from Nerinx Hall in 1960 before making it big in Hollywood. She later married and divorced playwright Neil Simon and starred in several of his plays, including *Only When I Laugh* and *The Goodbye Girl.*

McDonald, Michael

★ 946 Highmont Drive

A native of Ferguson, Missouri, Michael McDonald played with the rock group Steely Dan (who took their name from the book *Naked Lunch* by fellow St. Louisan William S. Burroughs) in the early 1970s. He was also successful as the singer for the Doobie Brothers from 1974 to 1982. The Doobie Brothers had hits with "What a Fool Believes" and "Minute by Minute" while McDonald was singing lead. He lived in this home in the 1950s.

McFerrin, Robert, Sr.

★ Sumner High School, 4248 Cottage Avenue

Baritone Robert McFerrin Sr. took classical voice lessons at Sumner High School. In 1955 he became the Metropolitan Opera's first African American male soloist. After touring and teaching, he returned to St. Louis in 1973.

McGwire, Mark

★ Busch Stadium, southwest corner of Broadway and Walnut Street

With a swing of his bat at Busch Stadium on September 8, 1998, Cardinals first baseman Mark McGwire hit home run number sixty-two, breaking the thirty-seven-year record held by Roger Maris. Caught up in the excitement, he failed to touch first base and had to go back and touch the bag. After rounding the bases, McGwire hugged his son, the Cubs' Sammy Sosa, Roger Maris's children, and FOX television announcer Joe Buck. At 341 feet, the record-setting home run was McGwire's shortest of the season.

The stadium was torn down after the 2005 playoffs, and a new Busch Stadium was built just to the south of the old grounds.

* 750 S. Hanley Road

Cardinals slugger Mark McGwire lived at 750 S. Hanley in the Claytonian Apartments in 1998, when he smashed Roger Maris's home run record.

McLuhan, Marshall

* 4343 McPherson Avenue

Marshall McLuhan, who wrote the book *The Medium Is the Massage* and coined the phrase "The medium is the message," lived at 4343 McPherson Avenue around 1938 or 1939. He taught in the English department at Saint Louis University for six years starting in 1938.

He also introduced the term "global village."

In addition to writing numerous scholarly books, he appeared as himself in the Woody Allen film *Annie Hall*.

* Jefferson Arms Hotel, 415 N. Tucker Boulevard

Media guru and author Marshall McLuhan and his wife, Corinne, spent their wedding night in this hotel in 1939.

Mead, Shepherd

* 6313 Waterman Boulevard

Author Shepherd Mead lived at this house from his birth in 1914 until about 1936. He attended Country Day High School and Washington University. His 1951 book *How to Succeed in Business Without Really Trying* was adapted to a Broadway musical with songs from Frank Loesser in 1961.

Meet Me in St. Louis

★ 5135 Kensington Avenue

St. Louis is home to one of the most famous addresses in movie history, 5135 Kensington Avenue. This is where Judy Garland lived in the 1944 classic film *Meet Me in St. Louis*.

Time magazine rated the film one of the top one hundred movies of all time. It was nominated for four Academy Awards.

In the movie, Garland plays the role of seventeen-year-old Esther Smith, whose family lives in St. Louis in 1903 but is about to move to New York. An important subplot includes Esther's fondness for "The Boy Next Door":

> But he doesn't know I exist
>
> No matter how I may persist
>
> So it's clear to see there's no hope for me
>
> Though I live at 5135 Kensington Avenue
>
> And he lives at 5133

Meet Me in St. Louis was based on a series of stories by writer Sally Benson published in *The New Yorker*. Benson's family did live at 5135 Kensington Avenue during the 1904 World's Fair and later moved to New York. The actual house, not shown in the movie, has been demolished.

5135 Kensington Avenue in 1917.
Halftone, 1917. Courtesy of *St. Louis Magazine*. MHS Library.

Merrick, David

★ Central High School, 3616 N. Garrison Street

While attending Central High School in the late 1920s, future Broadway producer David Merrick often played hooky and went to the movies. On September 29, 1927, a tornado ripped through his school, killing five girls and injuring sixteen other students. Merrick, however, was safe inside the movie theater. Show business, he said, saved his life.

The school closed in 1984, but the building is still there.

★ The Muny, Forest Park

In the early 1930s, a young David Margulois sold ice cream and soda at the Muny, St. Louis's large outdoor theater. After changing his name to David Merrick, he went on to produce some of the biggest shows in Broadway history: *42nd Street*; *Hello, Dolly!*; *Cactus Flower*; *Irma La Douce*; and *Gypsy*.

Merrick said he disliked St. Louis so much he refused to fly TWA because its planes often landed in St. Louis.

★ United Hebrew Temple, 225 S. Skinker Boulevard

Broadway producer and native St. Louisan David Merrick and his wife, Leonore, were married at the United Hebrew Temple on January 16, 1938.

The building is now used as the Missouri Historical Society's Library and Research Center.

United Hebrew Temple.
Photograph by W. C. Persons, ca. 1927. MHS Photographs and Prints.

Minor, Virginia Louisa

* Old Courthouse, 11 N. 4th Street

Womens' suffrage leader and Civil War relief worker Virginia Louisa Minor claimed her civil rights were violated when she was denied voter registration for the 1872 election. Her case eventually went to the Supreme Court in 1874, where she lost the decision.

Missouri School for the Blind

* Chestnut Street between 6th and 7th Streets

In 1860, students at the Missouri School for the Blind became the first in the United States to read and write using the Braille system. The school has since relocated to 3815 Magnolia Avenue.

Moorehead, Agnes

* 4531 McPherson Avenue

As a child, Agnes Moorehead lived at 4531 McPherson Avenue in the early 1900s. Her father was pastor of the First Presbyterian Church. She danced with the St. Louis Municipal Theatre Association, locally known as the Muny. She later enjoyed a successful acting career and appeared in Orson Welles's masterpiece *Citizen Kane* and as the character Endora in the television show *Bewitched*.

Mullett, A. B.

* Old Post Office, 815 Olive Street

The Old Post Office, which opened in 1884, was designed by A. B. Mullett, who also designed the Old Executive Office Building next to the White House in Washington, D.C. The Old Post Office has undergone a $35 million renovation and now houses various tenants.

See also French, Daniel Chester.

Murray, Bill

★ 2022 Cherokee Street

Actor Bill Murray and an elephant filmed a scene from the 1996 movie *Larger Than Life* on the sidewalk in front of the shops at 2022 Cherokee Street.

Musial, Stan

★ Fairgrounds Hotel, 3644 Natural Bridge Road

Cardinals slugger Stan Musial arrived in St. Louis at Union Station in 1941. He lived at the Fairgrounds Hotel for the next several years. Because the hotel was so close to Sportsman's Park, many ballplayers stayed there. Fans used to gather in the hotel lobby to see or hopefully meet the players.

This site is now the Fairgrounds Park Place apartments.

St. Louis Cardinals fielder Stan Musial.
Photograph by Massie, Missouri Resources Division, ca. 1950. MHS Photographs and Prints.

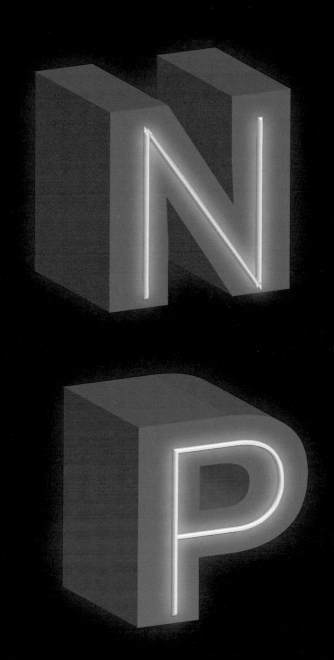

National Lampoon's Vacation -
Pulitzer, Joseph

National Lampoon's Vacation

* Poplar Street Bridge

The fictional Griswold family, played by actors including Chevy Chase and Beverly D'Angelo, drove over the Poplar Street Bridge going west in the movie *National Lampoon's Vacation*. There is a shot of the Gateway Arch and Highway 40 in the film.

Nelly

* University City High School, 7401 Balson Avenue

Rapper Cornell "Nelly" Haynes Jr. graduated from University City High School in 1993. Bursting onto the scene in 2001, he has won Grammy, Billboard Music, and American Music awards for his unique style of rap music.

* Tivoli Theatre, 6350 Delmar Boulevard

St. Louis native Nelly brought the premiere of his film *The Longest Yard* to the Tivoli Theatre on May 22, 2005. The rapper-turned-actor and other stars of the film, such as Burt Reynolds, Chris Rock, and Adam Sandler, strolled down a red carpet and greeted fans on the Loop.

Peck, Gregory

* Creve Coeur Park, 2143 Creve Coeur Mill Road

In an interview on KMOX Radio, the late actor Gregory Peck remembered playing at Creve Coeur Park when visiting relatives in the St. Louis area.

Philbin, Regis

★ 1 Memorial Drive

Here at KMOV Channel 4 in 1971, *Regis Philbin's Saturday Night in St. Louis* aired and gave the CBS affiliate the ratings necessary to win its time slot over *Saturday Night Live*. Philbin commuted from Los Angeles to St. Louis for the weekly broadcast.

See also Buck, Jack; Buck, Joe; Caray, Harry; Costas, Bob; Dierdorf, Dan.

Phillips, Stone

★ Parkway West High School, 14653 Clayton Road

Dateline NBC news correspondent Stone Phillips was voted "most athletic boy" in 1973 during his senior year at Parkway West High School. The future television star also scored big on the football field while in high school. He played quarterback for the Parkway West Longhorns.

Planes, Trains and Automobiles

★ Eads Bridge

In the 1987 movie *Planes, Trains and Automobiles,* actors Steve Martin and John Candy are in a bus heading east from Jefferson City to St. Louis. Strangely, the bus enters Missouri over the Eads Bridge from the west.

* Lambert-St. Louis International Airport

In one scene from the 1987 movie *Planes, Trains and Automobiles*, Steve Martin gets into a profanity-laced tirade with a car rental agent at Lambert. He is then punched in the face outside the main terminal.

Planter's Hotel

* Southwest corner of 4th and Pine Streets

The Planter's Hotel was built on this location in 1840 and was considered one of the finest in the West. Hotel guest Charles Dickens wrote in 1842, "It is an excellent house, and the proprietors have most bountiful notions of providing the creature comforts."

Abraham Lincoln, Jefferson Davis, Andrew Jackson, Henry Clay, and William F. Cody are also among the hotel's notable guests.

The hotel closed in 1922.

See also Davis, Jefferson; Dickens, Charles.

Poage, George

* Near Francis Field, northeast corner of Big Bend and Forsyth Boulevards (formerly south side of "New Gymnasium" at World's Fair)

George Poage was the first African American to both participate and medal in the modern Olympic Games. Poage won bronze medals in the

Poage, George cont'd

200-meter hurdle race and the 400-meter race, which were held here alongside the World's Fair Olympic Stadium in 1904. After the Olympics, Poage taught at Sumner High School.

Finish of the 200-meter hurdle race at the 1904 Olympics. George Poage finished in third place.
Photograph by Jessie Tarbox Beals, 1904. MHS Photographs and Prints.

Pontiac

★ Southeast corner of Broadway and Walnut Street

In 1769 this was the outskirts of young St. Louis. Indian leader Pontiac was buried here after being killed in Cahokia, Illinois, by a member of the

Peoria tribe. Pontiac was one of the most successful Indian military leaders; today, a city in Michigan and a make of car bear his name.

Pope John Paul II

* Edward Jones Dome (formerly TWA Dome), 701 Convention Plaza

Pope John Paul II celebrated what would be his last mass in the United States inside the TWA Dome (now the Edward Jones Dome) before 100,000 people on January 27, 1999.

Presidential debates

* Washington University Athletic Center, northeast corner of Big Bend and Forsyth Boulevards

Is St. Louis the debate capital? Washington University in St. Louis has been chosen to host the presidential debates four times (1992, 1996, 2000, 2004), more than any other university in the country.

In 1996 the debate among President Bill Clinton, Bob Dole, and Ross Perot was canceled because the number of debates was reduced from three to two.

Price, Vincent

* 6320 Forsyth Boulevard

Born in 1911, horror-movie star Vincent Price and his well-to-do family lived at 6320 Forsyth Boulevard. His dad was an executive with the National Candy Company. Price lived in the house on Forsyth until he left for Yale University.

His more memorable film appearances include *House of Wax* and *Edward Scissorhands*. He had several voice roles in film and television, including Michael Jackson's video for "Thriller."

Prince, Bob

* Chase Park Plaza (formerly Chase Hotel), 212 N. Kingshighway Boulevard

Jack Buck wrote in his 1997 memoir: "My favorite story about [Pittsburgh Pirates announcer Bob] Prince occurred at the old Chase Hotel in St. Louis, where most of the visiting teams stayed. . . .

"At the end of the pool the hotel windows are about a story and a half high. Some of the Pirate players were sitting around the pool, and their second baseman, Bill Mazeroski, said to Prince, 'Do you think you could dive out of that window into the pool?' The window was about 15 feet from the water across the deck.

"Prince said, 'Hell yeah, I could do that.' The players put up $100 and dared him to do it. Prince went into the hotel, appeared at the window, dove in and just made it. He almost wiped out on the deck. Harold Koplar, who owned the Chase, went crazy when he found out about it. He put cages in front of all the windows so nobody would try it again."

Pulitzer, Joseph

★ North leg of Gateway Arch (formerly 116–118 Chestnut Street)

Joseph Pulitzer, one of the most important figures in journalism, got his start in 1868 as a reporter for the *Westliche Post,* a German-language newspaper.

★ Old Courthouse, 11 N. 4th Street

Joseph Pulitzer, for whom the Pulitzer Prize is named, bought a bankrupt newspaper at auction on the steps of the Old Courthouse in 1878 and turned it into the *St. Louis Post-Dispatch.*

Old Courthouse in St. Louis.
Photograph by W. C. Persons, 1920s. MHS Photographs and Prints.

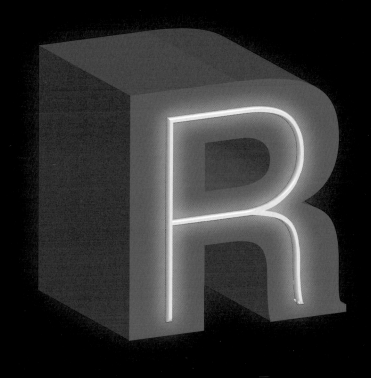

Ramis, Harold - Roosevelt, Franklin D.

Ramis, Harold

* Zeta Beta Tau fraternity house, Washington University, 7020 Forsyth Boulevard

The cowriter of 1978's raucous comedy *Animal House* was likely inspired by his own frat-boy days at the Zeta Beta Tau fraternity house at Washington University. Ramis graduated from Washington University in 1966. He is also known for acting in movies such as *Stripes* and *Ghostbusters* and cowriting and directing *Groundhog Day* and *Analyze This*.

Ray, John

* Grapevine Tavern, 1982 Arsenal Street

In January 1968, John Ray and his sister, Carol Pepper, opened the Grapevine Tavern at 1982 Arsenal Street. It served as a distribution point for the American Independent Party's "George Wallace for President" campaign literature. On April 4, 1968, their brother James Earl Ray assassinated the Reverend Dr. Martin Luther King Jr. in Memphis.

James Earl Ray had escaped from the Missouri State Penitentiary in 1967 and admitted visiting St. Louis after the escape. The United States House of Representatives Select Committee on Assassinations believed circumstantial evidence indicated King's murder may have been the result of a conspiracy with ties to the Grapevine Tavern.

Reagan, Ronald

* Sportsman's Park, 2901 N. Grand Avenue

In 1952, Harry Caray and Ronald Reagan broadcast two innings of a Cardinals game together. Reagan was in town to plug his latest movie,

Reagan, Ronald cont'd

The Winning Team, in which he played former Cardinals player Grover Cleveland Alexander.

The two would meet again in a Wrigley Field broadcast booth about thirty years later, when Caray was the Cubs' broadcaster and Reagan was the president of the United States.

Sportsman's Park is now the Herbert Hoover Boys Club.

See also Caray, Harry.

*   Renaissance Hotel (formerly Statler-Hilton Hotel), 822 Washington Avenue

Ronald Reagan, then a famous movie and television personality, spoke to an overflow crowd in the ballroom of the Statler-Hilton Hotel on January 23, 1962.

"What many liberals overlook," he said, "is the tendency of even the best government programs to take on weight and gain momentum. As we have taken every welfare problem to the central government for solution, we have seen the creation of a permanent structure of government so big and so complex that it is virtually beyond the control of Congress . . . certainly it is self-perpetuating."

Revels, Reverend Hiram R.

*   Corner of 7th Street and Washington Avenue

Rev. Hiram R. Revels served as pastor of the African Methodist Church at the corner of 7th Street and Washington Avenue in 1852. He later became the first African American to serve as a U.S. senator. The Mississippi legislature chose him to fill the seat once occupied by Jefferson Davis.

Rickey, Branch

★ 5802 Westminster Place

Baseball executive Branch Rickey lived at 5802 Westminster Place while working in the front office of the St. Louis Cardinals from 1925 to 1942. Rickey originated baseball's farm system and introduced black athletes into the major leagues.

In 1945, he became the first executive to break baseball's color line by signing Jackie Robinson to the Brooklyn Dodgers, the major league's first African American player.

The site is now a vacant lot.

Branch Rickey.
Photograph by J. C. Strauss, 1922. MHS Photographs and Prints.

Rockettes

B ! 5

∗   Missouri Theatre, 634 N. Grand Boulevard

The world-famous Radio City Rockettes started as the Missouri Rockets at the Missouri Theatre at 634 N. Grand Boulevard in 1925. They danced here for at least three years before moving to Radio City Music Hall and becoming the Rockettes in 1932.

The Missouri Theatre closed down in 1957.

Rombauer, Irma

D ! 5

∗   5712 Cabanne Avenue

Irma Rombauer, author of *The Joy of Cooking*, lived at 5712 Cabanne Avenue from 1931 to 1955. A widow, Rombauer self-published her book to make ends meet during the Depression.

The book became an American classic, selling more than 14 million copies before the end of the century.

Rombauer died in 1962.

Roosevelt, Franklin D.

* 18th and Market Streets

A parade touring the future grounds for the Gateway Arch began here at 9:30 a.m. on October 14, 1936. The Roosevelts and Vice President Harry S. Truman all participated in the parade, riding down Market Street in a convertible. President Roosevelt spoke at a platform that was set up at 13th and Market Streets.

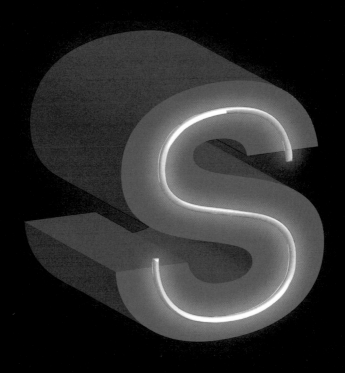

Scott, Dred - Stars Park

Scott, Dred

★   Old Courthouse, 11 N. 4th Street

The slave Dred Scott and his wife, Harriet, first sued for their freedom here. Their case went all the way to the U.S. Supreme Court, where the Scotts lost. This infamous decision led to sectional conflict and became a cause of the Civil War. It remains one of the most significant court decisions in U.S. history.

Scott, Harriet

★   Near 8th and Olive Streets

Harriet Scott was a slave who, along with her husband, Dred, first sued for her freedom in 1846. Their case resulted in a national debate and led to the Civil War.

Harriet died June 17, 1876, approximately eighteen years after her husband's death. At the time of her death, she was in the home of her daughter and son-in-law, which was about one block away from her own home.

Shange, Ntozake

★   15 Windermere Place

The house at 15 Windermere Place is the girlhood home of Ntozake Shange, who rose to national prominence after the 1975 production of her play, *For Colored Girls Who Have Considered Suicide/When the Rainbow Is Enuf*. The play was a hit on Broadway and on television.

Shange's semi-autobiographical 1985 novel *Betsey Brown* is set in the neighborhood of her home and describes an African American family

Shange, Ntozake cont'd

dealing with desegregation. Shange was bused to an integrated school, and she experienced racism and harassment there. However, such creative minds as Miles Davis, Josephine Baker, Chuck Berry, and W. E. B. Dubois were frequent guests at her family's home, and they surely helped create a refuge from her difficult school life.

Shelley, J. D.

* 4600 Labadie Avenue

J. D. Shelley bought a house at 4600 Labadie Avenue in 1939 for his family. However, neighbors cited a covenant barring its sale to "persons not of Caucasian race." In 1948 the U.S. Supreme Court ruled in favor of Shelley (*Shelley v. Kraemer*) and declared restrictive covenants limiting access to property on the basis of race were not legally enforceable.

The home was declared a National Historic Landmark in 1990.

J. D. Shelley residence, 4600 Labadie Avenue.
Photograph by David Schultz, 1993.
MHS Photographs and Prints.

Shenker, Morris

* Merchants Laclede Building, southwest corner of 4th and Olive Streets

Morris Shenker, attorney for Teamsters president Jimmy Hoffa, had an office in the Merchants Laclede Building. He also represented leading rack-eteers in St. Louis and owned the Dunes Casino in Las Vegas.

Sherman, William Tecumseh

* Jefferson Barracks, 533 Grant Road

General William T. Sherman was stationed at Jefferson Barracks military base in 1850.

* Locust Street between 10th and 11th Streets

Union general William Tecumseh Sherman moved to St. Louis in March 1861, as he describes in his memoir: "Mrs. Sherman and I gathered our family and effects together, started for St. Louis March 27th, where we rented of Mr. Lucas the house on Locust Street, between Tenth and Eleventh, and occupied it on the 1st of April."

* 5th and Locust Streets

Union general William Tecumseh Sherman worked in downtown St. Louis in April 1861, as he describes in his memoir: "In the latter part of March, I was duly elected president of the Fifth Street Railroad, and entered on the discharge of my duties April 1, 1861. We had a central office on the corner of Fifth and Locust. . . ."

Sherman, William Tecumseh cont'd

However, the Civil War started two weeks later, and Sherman left St. Louis to lead Union forces as a general. Under his direction, soldiers burned Atlanta. Much of his action was chronicled in the book and the movie Gone with the Wind.

He was famous for stating, "War is hell."

Sincoff, Jerry

A

50

* American Zinc Building, northeast corner of 4th and Walnut Streets

St. Louis architect Jerry Sincoff of the firm Hellmuth, Obata + Kassabaum designed the 1967 American Zinc Company Building at 4th and Walnut Streets. The stainless steel building pays tribute to its original owner's metals industry and not, as is sometimes believed, the nearby stainless steel Gateway Arch. The building is now the southernmost part of a renovated hotel.

Sincoff was also responsible for project development, from design to occupancy, of one of the country's most popular museums, the Smithsonian National Air and Space Museum in Washington, D.C. The museum, which opened July 4, 1976, was also designed by Gyo Obata and Chih-Chen Jen.

Skouras, Spyros

F

8

* 6950 Pershing Avenue

Movie producer Spyros Skouras lived at 6950 Pershing Avenue in the 1920s. A Greek immigrant, Skouras worked his way up from restaurant busboy to owner of a chain of thirty-seven theaters, including the Tivoli on Delmar Boulevard. By 1942, Skouras was the president of 20th Century Fox and one of the most powerful executives in Hollywood. He acquired the rights to Cinemascope and used the widescreen process to produce such films as *The Robe*, starring Richard Burton.

His career in Hollywood declined after his studio released *Cleopatra*, an overbudget film that did not meet expectations.

Smith, Huston

* 205 S. Skinker Boulevard

Huston Smith, a Washington University professor and son of Methodist missionaries, helped acquire the property at 205 S. Skinker Boulevard for the Vedanta Society of St. Louis. Smith served as chairman of the Vedanta Society in 1952 when the property was purchased.

Smith taught world religions at Washington University in the 1940s and 1950s. He was an apprentice to Swami Satprakashananda, a Hindu teacher in St. Louis.

It was in St. Louis that Smith wrote *The Religions of Man*, later revised as *The World's Religions*, which since its 1958 release has sold more than 2.5 million copies. The book is available in twelve languages. Today, Smith is widely viewed as the leading authority on the world's religions.

Smith, Luther Ely

* 21 Waterman Place (formerly 5321 Waterman Boulevard)

Luther Ely Smith served on the national commission establishing a memorial to George Rogers Clark in Indiana, and that's where he got the idea to build a memorial in St. Louis to Thomas Jefferson. He, more than anyone

Smith, Luther Ely cont'd

else, pushed for what became the Jefferson National Expansion Memorial, also known as the Gateway Arch.

Smith lived at 5321 Waterman Boulevard in 1949. Smith held no elective office and died in 1952, thirteen years before the Arch was completed.

★   4th and Market Streets, across from the Arch

St. Louisan Luther Ely Smith came up with the idea to put a national monument on the Mississippi River in downtown St. Louis. Advertising pioneer William Cheever D'Arcy served as chairman of the Jefferson National Expansion Memorial Committee. Eero Saarinen designed the Arch. None of the men lived to see the landmark; however, the park across the street is named after Smith.

See also D'Arcy, William Cheever.

Soldan High School

★   918 N. Union Boulevard

Soldan High School opened in 1909 at 918 N. Union Boulevard. Its list of former students includes actress Virgina Mayo (*The Secret Life of Walter Mitty*), U.S. senator Thomas Hennings, and author A. E. Hotchner (*Papa Hemingway*).

Around the year 1922, Clark Clifford and William McChesney Martin Jr. were doubles partners on the Soldan High School tennis team. Later, Clifford became White House counsel for President Harry S. Truman, while Martin served Truman and five other presidents as chairman of the Federal Reserve.

See also Clifford, Clark; Hotchner, A. E.; Martin, William McChesney, Jr. and Sr.

Spinks,
Leon and Michael

★ Darst-Webbe housing project, 1241 Hickory Street

Boxing brothers Leon and Michael Spinks grew up in both the Pruitt-Igoe and the Darst-Webbe housing projects, the latter of which was located at 1241 Hickory Street. Both also won gold medals in the 1976 Olympics in Montreal.

Leon later defeated Muhammad Ali to win the heavyweight championship, but he lost it in his rematch with Ali. Michael also earned the heavyweight title by beating Larry Holmes. However, he lost his boxing title to Mike Tyson.

Leon later moved to Nebraska and found work as a janitor, and Michael moved to the East Coast.

Darst-Webbe
Public Housing.
Photograph by Community
Development Agency photographer,
1971. MHS Photographs and Prints.

Stagger Lee

* 911 N. Tucker Boulevard

On Christmas night 1895, "Stack" Lee Shelton shot Billy Lyons at a now-defunct saloon located at present-day 11th and Delmar (now called Convention Plaza). The incident has become something of a legend in music circles.

Through the years, "Stack" has evolved into "Stagger," and songs inspired by "Stagger Lee" have been performed or recorded by Neil Diamond, the Grateful Dead, Duke Ellington, the Clash, the Isley Brothers, the Righteous Brothers, and hundreds of others.

Stagger Lee lived at 911 N. Tucker Boulevard. The building still stands.

Stars Park

★ Near the corner of Compton Avenue and Market Street

Baseball's Negro League St. Louis Stars, previously the St. Louis Giants, played at a stadium here from 1921 to 1931. Hall of Famer James "Cool Papa" Bell played for the Stars when they won the Negro League National Championship in 1931.

The site is now occupied by the Vashon Recreation Center.

See also Bell, James "Cool Papa."

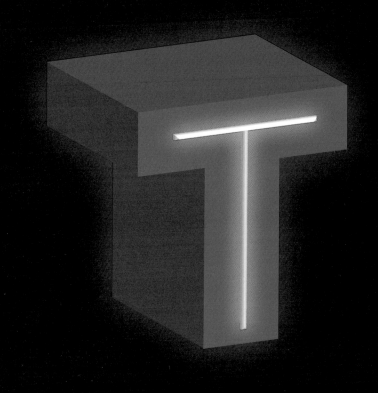

Taylor, Zachary - Twain, Mark

Taylor, Zachary

* Jefferson Barracks, 533 Grant Road

Future president Zachary Taylor was commander of troops at Jefferson Barracks military base in 1836.

Thomas, Clarence

* 1 Greendale Drive

Supreme Court justice Clarence Thomas lived at 1 Greendale Drive from 1977 to 1979. At the time, he worked at Monsanto Company as a lawyer dealing with pesticide, fungicide, and rodenticide law.

Tilden, Samuel

* Southeast corner of Pine and 4th Streets

The Merchants' Exchange Building served as a convention hall in 1876, where Democrats nominated Samuel Tilden, governor of New York, to be their candidate for president. Tilden got more votes than Rutherford B. Hayes in the November election. However, the votes in four states (Florida, Louisiana, South Carolina, and Oregon) were disputed. An ad hoc committee of eight Republicans and seven Democrats voted eight to seven to give Hayes the twenty electoral votes he needed to win the electoral college 185 to 184.

A hotel now stands on the site.

Truman, Harry S.

* Union Station, 1820 Market Street

Perhaps the most famous political photograph of the twentieth century shows Harry S. Truman holding up a copy of the *Chicago Daily Tribune* with the erroneous headline "Dewey Defeats Truman." The newspaper's Washington correspondent told the paper's editors on election night it would be a safe bet to print the headline. The final vote count proved otherwise.

The victorious President Truman was aboard a train heading from Missouri to Washington, D.C., the next day, November 3, 1948. When he was handed a copy of the paper during a stop at Union Station, he held it up and grinned before the cameras.

Harry S. Truman.
Photograph by Chase-Statler Photographers, 1944. MHS Photographs and Prints.

TUMS Building

* 301 S. 4th Street

The TUMS Building is the only place in the world where TUMS antacid tablets are manufactured. The plant has been operating in St. Louis since the early 1900s.

See also Lewis, A. H.

Turner, Tina

* Maternity ward, Barnes-Jewish Hospital (formerly Barnes Hospital), 216 S. Kingshighway Boulevard

Anna Mae Bullock moved to St. Louis in 1956, when she was sixteen years old.

> She attended Sumner High School and then began to sing in clubs with local musician Ike Turner, who would become her husband.

Early in her career she sang at night, and cleaned and cared for babies in the maternity ward of Barnes Hospital during the day. Later known as Tina Turner, she was one of the top recording artists in the 1980s, with such hits as "Private Dancer" and "What's Love Got to Do with It."

Twain, Mark

* Mansion House Building, 300 N. 4th Street

This is where Mark Twain worked at a newspaper, the *Evening News and Intelligencer*, in 1853. Twain wrote some of the best-known works in American literature, including *The Adventures of Tom Sawyer* and *Adventures of Huckleberry Finn*, the latter of which includes some description of St. Louis: "The fifth night we passed St. Louis, and it was like the whole world lit up. In St. Petersburg they used to say there was twenty or thirty thousand people in St. Louis, but I never believed it till I see that wonderful spread of lights at two o'clock that still night. There wasn't a sound there; everybody was asleep."

The Mansion House Apartments stand on this site today.

* Cole (formerly Wash) and 4th Streets

If you stand on Interstate 70 just east of the northern edge of the Edward Jones Dome, you will find the spot where Mark Twain lived at the corner of Wash and Fourth Streets in 1854. He boarded with the Paveys, a family from Hannibal, Missouri.

* 219 Pine Street (formerly 35 Pine Street)

Mark Twain and Ulysses Grant had a St. Louis connection: In 1859, Grant was a junior partner in the real estate and rent collection firm Boggs and Grant. With business lagging, Grant passed the time hanging out nearby at the business owned by Twain's brother-in-law, William Moffett.

Later, the two almost met in battle near Florida, Missouri, during the brief period that Twain carried a gun for the Confederacy.

Twain idolized Grant and later published Grant's memoirs.

See also Grant, Ulysses S.

* Jefferson Barracks, 533 Grant Road

The Civil War, specifically an incident related to Jefferson Barracks, ended Samuel Clemens's career as a steamboat pilot. In 1861 he was a passenger in a boat that did not at first heed the signal to halt while passing Jefferson Barracks just below St. Louis on the Mississippi River. A cannon blast from shore caused some damage to the pilothouse and knocked the pilot to the ground. Clemens took the wheel and turned the boat around. He subsequently retired from piloting steamboats, writing, "I am not anxious to get up into a glass perch and be shot at by either side. I'll go home and reflect."

Clemens, using the pen name Mark Twain, would go on to become one of America's greatest writers.

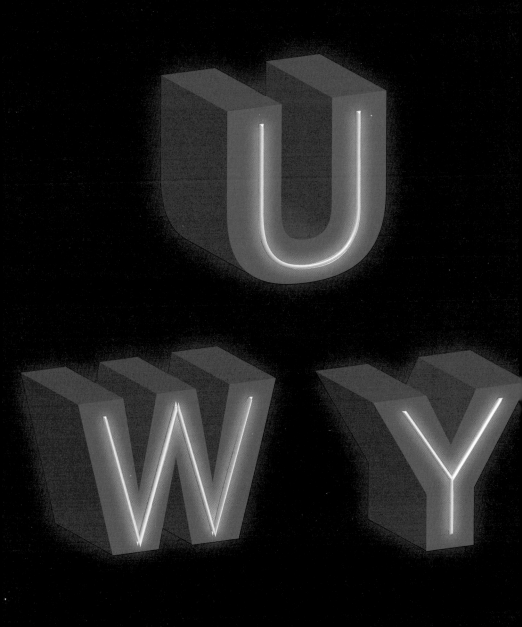

U2 - Young, Cy

U2

* Washington University's Graham Chapel, One Brookings Drive

On April 7, 1981, a young band named U2 performed a concert of about twelve songs at the Graham Chapel on the campus of Washington University. Today, U2 is one of rock's biggest acts.

Wainwright Building

* 705 Chestnut Street

The 1890 Wainwright Building is widely considered America's first skyscraper. St. Louis brewer Ellis Wainwright commissioned Chicago architect Louis Sullivan for the project. Sullivan imagined the design while taking a walk down Michigan Avenue and reportedly ran back to his office in the Auditorium Building to quickly sketch his plan. The architect cleverly recessed the building's horizontal spandrels and windows and thus made the building's vertical red brick pilasters more distinct. This had the effect of exaggerating the building's height. A departure from other buildings of its day, the Wainwright was called "height triumphant" by Frank Lloyd Wright, a student of Sullivan's.

Still the subject of numerous books and documentaries, the Wainwright Building's place in the pantheon of important American buildings is assured.

Wainwright Building, 709 Chestnut Street.
Photograph by Emil Boehl, ca. 1907. MHS Photographs and Prints.

Walker, David Davis

★ 1520 Washington Avenue

President George W. Bush can trace his roots to this spot. In 1880, David Davis Walker started his wholesale dry goods business in downtown St. Louis, and by 1906 his company, Ely and Walker Dry Goods, was headquartered at 1520 Washington Avenue. Walker's son was George Herbert Walker, who fathered Dorothy Davis Walker, who bore President George Herbert Walker Bush, the father of President George Walker Bush.

★ North of Delmar Boulevard, between Grand Boulevard and Spring Avenue (formerly 53 Vandeventer Place)

The firm of Grable and Weber designed a home at 53 Vandeventer Place for David Davis Walker, the great-great-grandfather of President George W. Bush, in 1891. The street was demolished in 1948 to make way for the VA hospital.

★ 10 Hortense Place

David Davis Walker built a home at 10 Hortense Place in 1907. George W. Hellmuth designed the house. The building still stands.

Weaver, Earl

★ Beaumont High School, 3836 Natural Bridge Road

Earl Weaver , who managed the Baltimore Orioles from 1968 to 1982 and 1985 to 1986, was a member of Beaumont High School's 1944 baseball team.

See also Beaumont High School.

Earl Weaver's father cleaned the uniforms for the St. Louis Cardinals and Browns in the 1930s and 1940s. Thus, young Earl was able to watch as many as one hundred games per season. In 1944 he had tickets to all six World Series games between the Browns and the Cardinals.

Weaver also played on the local sandlots. In August 1946, he got three hits and stole a base in the Muny League all-star game sponsored by the *Globe-Democrat* newspaper at Fairgrounds Park.

Weaver's father sold newspapers as a kid with Bill DeWitt, who became owner of the Browns in the late 1940s. Earl Weaver turned down a Browns contract offer from DeWitt in 1948. Instead, Weaver signed with the Cardinals, although he never made it beyond the team's farm system. DeWitt's son Bill Jr. bought the Cardinals in 1995.

When the Browns became the Orioles after they moved to Baltimore, Weaver managed them to one of the best records in modern baseball. From 1968 through 1982 the Orioles had a .596 winning percentage. His teams finished first or second twelve times.

Weaver, Earl cont'd

Sportsman's Park was demolished in 1966 and is now the Herbert Hoover Boys Club.

*   City Hall, southwest corner of Tucker Boulevard and Market Street

Some may be surprised to learn who used to work for the City of St. Louis. Longtime Baltimore Orioles manager Earl Weaver installed parking meters in St. Louis in 1950. He also worked in the city's tax collection department in 1953.

St. Louis City Hall.
Photograph by A. W. Sanders, 1900–1904. MHS Photographs and Prints.

White, Jo Jo

* 2 Rutger Street

Jo Jo White grew up at 2 Rutger Street. Neighbors remember seeing a young White practicing basketball until 1 a.m. on the St. Henry parish playground in the early 1960s. St. Henry, at the intersection of California Avenue and Hickory Street until 1977, had the only basketball court in south St. Louis with night lights. "My parents thought I was up to no good staying out all night but I really was practicing my game," recalls White.

The practice paid off because White later became a two-time All-American at the University of Kansas and won a gold medal in basketball at the 1968 Olympics.

White was drafted by the Cincinnati Reds and the Dallas Cowboys but instead chose to play basketball with the Boston Celtics. He helped his team win the NBA Championship in 1974 and 1976 and was named an NBA All-Star seven times.

White Palace

* Cheshire Inn, 6300 Clayton Road

In the novel *White Palace* by St. Louisan Glenn Savan, young widower Max and friends attend a bachelor party at the Cheshire Inn on Clayton Road.

* Northwest corner of 18th and Olive Streets

In the movie *White Palace*, Max (James Spader) meets waitress Nora (Susan Sarandon) at the White Palace restaurant. The scene was filmed inside the real-life White Knight restaurant at the corner of 18th and Olive Streets.

* 1521 West Billon Avenue

In the movie *White Palace,* Nora (Susan Sarandon) lived at 1521 West Billon Avenue.

Whitman, Walt

* Eads Bridge

Walt Whitman made a three-month visit to his brother, Thomas, in St. Louis in 1879.

He wrote of the Eads Bridge: "It is indeed a structure of perfection and beauty unsurpassable, and I never tire of it."

Williams, Rose

* Church of St. Michael and St. George, 6345 Wydown Boulevard

Around 1935, after spreading a rumor that the rector of St. Michael and St. George Episcopal Church had "Jewish blood," Rose Williams, sister of playwright Tennessee Williams, was relieved of her teaching duties at the church's Sunday school. She later lived in a mental hospital and died in 1996.

Williams, Tennessee

* 4633 Westminster Place

Eight-year-old Tennessee Williams and his family moved to St. Louis in the summer of 1918, stayed briefly in a boarding house on Lindell Boulevard, and then moved to the apartments at 4633 Westminster Place. He later described the building as "dim" and "ugly."

> After Williams's success, the property's owner began calling the building the Glass Menagerie Apartments. However, the actual setting for the play *The Glass Menagerie* was in University City.

* 5 S. Taylor Avenue

In 1922, eleven-year-old Tennessee Williams and his family moved to the Lyndon Building on the corner of Laclede and Taylor Avenues. He used his

Williams, Tennessee cont'd

first typewriter here to create stories. He would become one of the most prominent playwrights in America.

* 5938 Cates Avenue

Playwright Tennessee Williams lived at 5938 Cates Avenue at the age of thirteen in 1924.

* Ben Blewett Junior High School, 5351 Enright Avenue

Playwright Tennessee Williams attended Ben Blewett Junior High School in 1924. He wrote stories and poetry for the school newspaper, but his father thought it was "a lot of foolishness." The younger Williams would later receive two Pulitzer Prizes for his writing.

After several other uses, the building is now vacant.

* 6254 Enright Avenue

Tennessee Williams and his family moved into a small apartment at 6254 Enright Avenue in June 1926 so that Tennessee could enter tenth grade at University City High School.

This building, now gone, was the setting for his 1944 play, *The Glass Menagerie.*

* University City High School, 7401 Balson Avenue

Tennessee Williams attended University City High School and graduated fifty-third in a class of eighty-three on June 13, 1929.

★ Rubicam Business School, 4931–4933 Delmar Boulevard

Tennessee Williams's real-life sister, Rose, and *The Glass Menagerie's* fictional Laura failed their typing classes at the Rubicam Business School. A then-nineteen-year-old Tennessee Williams and his sister took the same business course here in the summer of 1930.

★ International Shoe Company, 1501–1509 Washington Avenue

At his father's insistence, Tennessee Williams worked at the International Shoe Company warehouse on Washington Avenue after getting mediocre grades at the University of Missouri in Columbia. He started the job in 1932, and the work lasted about three years. He made sixty-five dollars a month, decent wages during the Depression.

The warehouse is where he met Jim Connor, who would become Jim O'Connor, the gentleman caller in *The Glass Menagerie*. Also, a fellow employee, Stanley Kowalski, would lend his name to a character in *A Streetcar Named Desire*.

The work experience was the inspiration for Williams's *Stairs to the Roof* in 1945.

Williams later said, "The two years I spent in that corporation were indescribable torment to me as an individual but of immense value to me as a writer for they gave me first-hand knowledge of what it means to be a small wage-earner in a hopelessly routine job."

The building is now the City Museum.

Williams, Tennessee cont'd

* Mercantile Library, 510 Locust Street

Even though he wrote *A Lovely Sunday for Creve Coeur,* playwright Tennessee Williams spent many Sundays in the early 1930s reading "voraciously" at the Mercantile Library at 510 Locust Street.

The building is still there, but the Mercantile Library is now located at the University of Missouri–St. Louis campus.

The Mercantile Library on the southwest corner of Broadway and Locust Street.
Halftone by Sanders, 1892. MHS Library.

* 6634 Pershing Avenue

Tennessee Williams and his family lived at 6634 Pershing Avenue around 1935. While here, he audited evening classes at Washington University. The building still exists.

Tennessee Williams as a member of the Washington University School Literary Magazine Staff.
Halftone, 1938. MHS Library.

* 42 Aberdeen Place

Tennessee Williams's family rented the house at 42 Aberdeen Place from 1937 to about 1940. He lived at the house when he wasn't studying at the University of Iowa. Williams described it as "a fine location." From this address he applied for work at KXOK, a new radio station owned by the *St. Louis Star-Times*.

See also Kline, Kevin.

* 53 Arundel Place

Tennessee Williams's mother, Edwina, lived at 53 Arundel Place in the 1940s, when Tennesse was an up-and-coming writer. In the basement, he worked on a screenplay about Louisiana governor Huey Long. He wrote letters from this address, claiming his mother monitored his phone calls from the house by listening in on the other line.

Williams, Tennessee cont'd

* 6360 Wydown Boulevard

Tennessee Williams's mother lived at 6360 Wydown in her later years in the 1950s. Tennessee, who modeled the character Amanda in *The Glass Menagerie* after Edwina, was very successful by this time. He stayed at his mother's home when visiting St. Louis. In 1955 he wrote a letter from this address, stating he was in St. Louis to visit "what remains of my family."

* Barnes-Jewish Hospital (formerly Barnes Hospital), 216 S. Kingshighway Boulevard

Tennessee Williams stayed in Barnes Hospital at 216 South Kingshighway in 1968 for psychiatric treatment. He referred to it as "Barnacle Hospital in the city of St. Pollution."

Winters, Shelley

* 1324 N. Newstead Avenue

Shelley Winters was born Shirley Schrift, the daughter of shoemaker Jonas Schrift, and grew up in a three-room ground-floor apartment on Newstead Avenue. The building was a four-story tenement. Winters became a star early in her life, participating in the Veiled Prophet pageant at the age of four before going on to star in fifty plays and more than one hundred films and television programs.

She won two Academy Awards, for her roles in *The Diary of Anne Frank* (1959) and *A Patch of Blue* (1965).

She died in 2006. The old Raskas (then Schreiber) Dairy building encompasses this address.

Wolfe, Thomas

* 5095 Cates Avenue (formerly Fairmont Avenue)

Everyone has heard the phrase "you can't go home again." It means the past can't be recovered and was the title of a book by author Thomas Wolfe, who lived at 5095 Fairmont Avenue for seven months in 1904, when he was four years old. Wolfe's mother ran a boardinghouse at this location, for visitors to the World's Fair. He later wrote about his family and his returning to this building in the epic novel *Look Homeward, Angel* (1929), a classic in American literature.

Woods, Tiger

* Shell gas station, Hanley Road near Wydown Boulevard

The longest drive of Tiger Woods's life started at a Clayton gas station. After the terrorist attacks of September 11, 2001, PGA officials cancelled the WGC-American Express Championship scheduled that week in St. Louis. With the nation's airports closed, Woods got into a car and filled it up at the Shell station on Hanley Road near Wydown Boulevard. Dressed in a T-shirt, jeans, and tennis shoes, Woods left St. Louis at 3:30 in the afternoon on Wednesday, September 12. He was headed back home to Florida with a good supply of water and protein bars. He drove alone. He arrived in Orlando—a distance of one thousand miles—at 6:30 the next morning.

Along the way, he decided the Tiger Woods Foundation needed to do more for the nation's kids. In February 2006, Woods dedicated the $25 million Tiger Woods Learning Center in a low-income neighborhood of Anaheim, California, which fulfilled, he said, his thoughts on that long trip from St. Louis to Orlando.

The site now houses a dry cleaning business.

World Series roommates

B 3

* Lindell Towers, 3745 Lindell Boulevard

The 1944 World Series featured the St. Louis Cardinals of the National League versus the St. Louis Browns of the American League. This posed a problem for the club's managers—Luke Sewell of the Browns and Billy Southworth of the Cardinals—who shared the same apartment at the Lindell Towers. During the regular season, one club was always on the road while the other club was at home. Sewell and Southworth even split the same closet for their clothes, although their wives each had their own.

During the World Series, Southworth stayed at a nearby hotel. However, the two managers drove home together after each game.

Strangely enough, Leo Durocher, manager of the Brooklyn Dodgers, lived in the same building during the offseason with his then-wife, Grace, a clothing executive in St. Louis.

Young, Chic

★ 2148 Oregon Avenue

Four years on the art staff of the McKinley High School yearbook were just the beginning for cartoonist Murat Bernard "Chic" Young, who grew up at 2148 Oregon Avenue. In 1930, eleven years after graduating from high school, Young created the *Blondie* comic strip. Although Young died in 1973, *Blondie* is now written by his son and read by millions in dozens of countries.

The comic strip inspired movies, television shows, and the dagwood, a huge sandwich frequently made by Blondie's husband, Dagwood Bumstead.

Young, Cy

★ League Park, 3836 Natural Bridge Road

Cy Young pitched his first game as a St. Louis Redbird on April 15, 1899, on this site, which is now the location of Beaumont High School. He earned the win as the Redbirds defeated the Cleveland Browns 10–1. Young pitched his way to a 26–16 record that season, but he did not keep his heart set in St. Louis. The American League's Boston Red Sox made him a better offer, and Young abandoned the St. Louis heat to pitch for Boston until he retired with more than five hundred victories at the age of forty-four.

Map A: *Downtown*

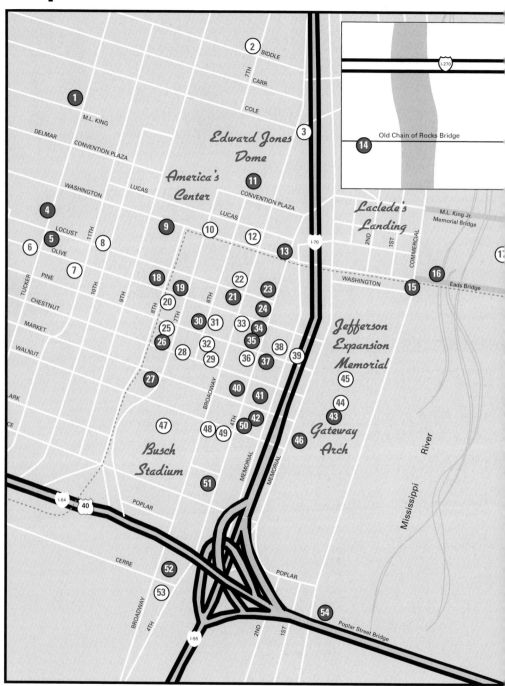

America's Center

Edward Jones Dome

Laclede's Landing

Jefferson Expansion Memorial

Gateway Arch

Busch Stadium

Mississippi River

Old Chain of Rocks Bridge

M.L. King Jr. Memorial Bridge

Eads Bridge

Poplar Street Bridge

1. Stagger Lee
911 N. Tucker Blvd.

2. Inge, William
1213 N. 7th St. (at Biddle St.)

3. Twain, Mark
Cole and 4th Sts.

4. Hornsby, Rogers; McLuhan, Marshall
415 N. Tucker Blvd.

5. Lindbergh, Charles
St. Louis Post-Dispatch building
306 N. Tucker Blvd.

6. American Legion
321 N. Tucker Blvd.

7. Eliot, T. S.
1104 Olive St.

8. Sherman, William Tecumseh
Locust St. between 10th and 11th Sts.

9. Reagan, Ronald
Renaissance Hotel
822 Washington Ave.

10. Revels, Reverend Hiram R.:
Corner of 7th St. and Washington Ave.

11. Pope John Paul II
Edward Jones Dome
701 Convention Plz.

12. Keckly, Elizabeth
5 Broadway (between Washington and Lucas Aves.)

13. Blackmun, Harry; Bradley, Bill
Missouri Athletic Club
405 Washington Ave.

14. *Escape from New York*
Old Chain of Rocks Bridge

15. Handy, W. C.
Beneath the Eads Bridge

16. Eliot, T. S.; *Planes, Trains and Automobiles*; Whitman, Walt
Eads Bridge

17. Benton, Thomas Hart
Bloody Island in the Mississippi River

18. French, Daniel Chester; Mullett, A. B.
Old Post Office
815 Olive St.

19. Clifford, Clark; Gephardt, Richard
705 Olive St.

20. Scott, Harriet
Near 8th and Olive Sts.

21. Williams, Tennessee
510 Locust St.

22. Sherman, William Tecumseh
5th and Locust Sts.

23. Martin, William McChesney, Jr. and Sr.
Northwest corner of 4th and Locust Sts.

24. Lindbergh, Charles; Twain, Mark
Corner of 4th and Locust Sts.

25. Dreiser, Theodore
708 Pine St.

26. Wainwright Building
709 Chestnut St.

27. Johnson, Philip
General American Life Building
700 Market St.

28. Missouri School for the Blind
Chestnut St. between 6th and 7th Sts.

29. Brandeis, Louis
North side of Chestnut St. near Broadway

30. Buck, Jack
Charlie Gitto's
207 N. 6th St.

31. Caray, Harry
210 N. 6th St.

32. D'Arcy, William Cheever
Pine and 6th Sts.

33. Clark, William
Southeast corner of Broadway and Olive St.

34. Lindbergh, Charles; Shenker, Morris
4th and Olive Sts.

35. Francis, David R.
Northwest corner of 4th and Pine Sts.

36. Dickens, Charles; Planter's Hotel
Southwest corner of 4th and Pine Sts.

37. Boston Red Sox; Tilden, Samuel
Adam's Mark Hotel
Southeast corner of Pine and 4th Sts.

38. Heron, M. W.
319 Pine St.

39. Twain, Mark
219 Pine St.

40. Brandeis, Louis; Minor, Virginia Louisa; Pulitzer, Joseph; Scott, Dred
Old Courthouse
11 N. 4th St.

41. Smith, Luther Ely
4th and Market Sts., across from Gateway Arch

42. Buck, Joe; Costas, Bob; Dierdorf, Dan; Philbin, Regis
1 Memorial Dr.

43. Hurt, William
Gateway Arch

44. Pulitzer, Joseph
North leg of Gateway Arch

45. Clark, William
Just north of Gateway Arch

46. Charbonneau, Jean Baptiste
Old Cathedral
209 Walnut St.

47. Boston Red Sox; McGwire, Mark
Southwest corner of
Broadway and Walnut St.

48. Pontiac
Southeast corner of
Broadway and Walnut St.

49. Fort San Carlos
4th and Walnut Sts.

50. Sincoff, Jerry
American Zinc Building
Northeast corner of 4th and Walnut Sts.

51. TUMS Building
301 S. 4th St.

52. Field, Eugene
634 S. Broadway

53. Grant, Ulysses S.
Southwest corner of 4th and Cerre Sts.

54. *National Lampoon's Vacation*
Poplar St. Bridge

Map B: *Midtown* *part 1*

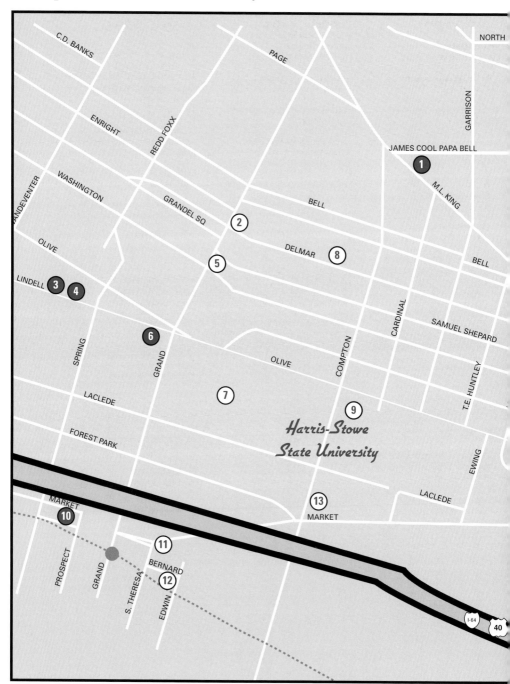

1. **Bell, James "Cool Papa"**
James Cool Papa Bell Ave.

2. **Berry, Chuck**
814 N. Grand Blvd.

3. **World Series roommates**
3745 Lindell Blvd.

4. **Inge, William**
3701 Lindell Blvd.

5. **Rockettes**
634 N. Grand Blvd.

6. **Bowdern, Father William**
St. Francis Xavier Church
3628 Lindell Blvd.

7. **Lyon, Nathaniel**
Camp Jackson
Bounded by Olive, Laclede, Ewing, and
Grand

8. **Chopin, Kate**
3317 Delmar Blvd.

9. **Baker, Josephine**
Harris-Stowe State University

10. **Ashe Arthur; Connors, Jimmy**
138th Infantry Armory
3676 Market St.

11. **First gas station**
412 S. Theresa Ave.

12. **Baker, Josephine**
2632 Bernard St.

13. **Stars Park**
Near Compton Ave. and Market St.

Map C: *Midtown* part 2

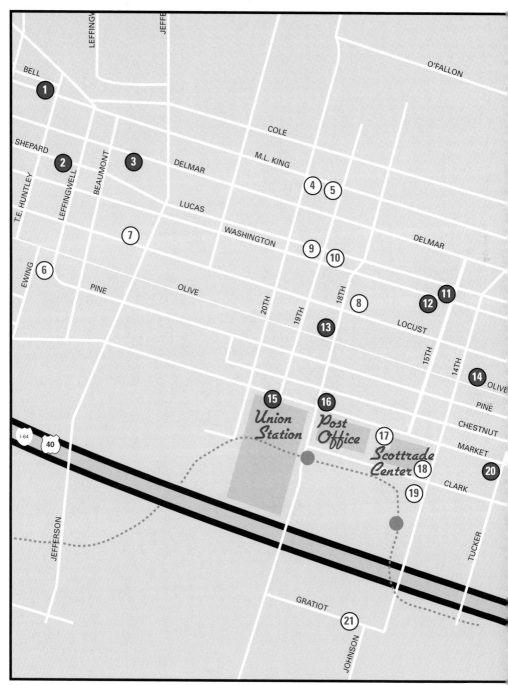

1. Foxx, Redd
2900 block of Bell Ave.

2. Foxx, Redd
Banneker School
2840 Samuel Shepard Dr.

3. Joplin, Scott
2658A Delmar Blvd.

4. Guillaume, Robert
Dr. Martin Luther King Dr. between 19th
and 20th Sts.

5. Guillaume, Robert
19th St. and Dr. Martin Luther King Dr.

6. Liston, Sonny
Pine St. and Ewing Ave.

7. Eliot, T. S.
2635 Locust St.

8. Brookings, Robert S.
Locust St. between 14th and 18th Sts.

9. Guillaume, Robert
1916 Lucas Pl.

10. Eliot, T. S.
19th St. and Washington Ave.

11. Guillaume, Robert; Williams, Tennessee
15th St. and Washington Ave.

12. Walker, David Davis
1520 Washington Ave.

13. *White Palace*
NW corner of 18th and Olive Sts.

14. Gilbert, Cass
St. Louis Public Library
1301 Olive St.

15. Baker, Josephine; Truman, Harry S.
Union Station
1820 Market St.

16. Roosevelt, Franklin D.
18th and Market Sts.

17. Liston, Sonny
1502 Market St.

18. Handy, W. C.
14th St. and Clark Ave.

19. "Frankie and Johnny"
212 Johnson St.

20. Bell, James "Cool Papa"; Weaver, Earl
City Hall
Tucker Blvd. and Market St.

21. Baker, Josephine
Gratiot St. near Johnson St.

Map D: *West Central City* *part 1*

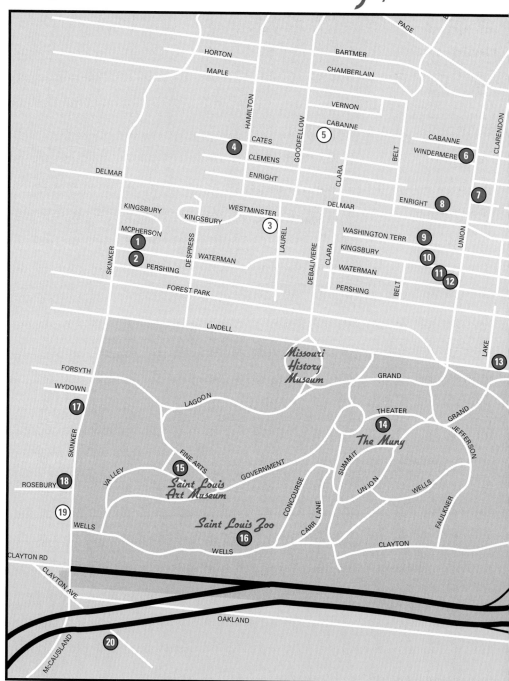

1. Inge, William
6168 McPherson Ave.

2. Eagleton, Thomas F.
6168 Waterman Blvd.

3. Rickey, Branch
5802 Westminster Pl.

4. Williams, Tennessee
5938 Cates Ave.

5. Rombauer, Irma
5712 Cabanne Ave.

6. Shange, Ntozake
15 Windermere Pl.

7. Soldan High School
918 N. Union Blvd.

8. Williams, Tennessee
Ben Blewett Junior High School
5351 Enright Ave.

9. Kann, Stan
29 Washington Terr.

10. Danforth, William H.
17 Kingsbury Blvd.

11. Edwards, Benjamin F.
10 Kingsbury Blvd.

12. Smith, Luther Ely
21 Waterman Pl.

13. Brookings, Robert S.
5125 Lindell Blvd.

14. Gregory, Dick; Merrick, David
The Muny, Forest Park

15. Gilbert, Cass
Saint Louis Art Museum
Forest Park
1 Fine Arts Drive

16. *Glass Menagerie, The*
Forest Park

17. Smith, Huston
205 S. Skinker Blvd.

18. Brock, Lou
665 S. Skinker Blvd.

19. Caray, Harry
825 S. Skinker Blvd.

20. Caray, Harry
Dewey School
6746 Clayton Ave.

Map E: *West Central City* part 2

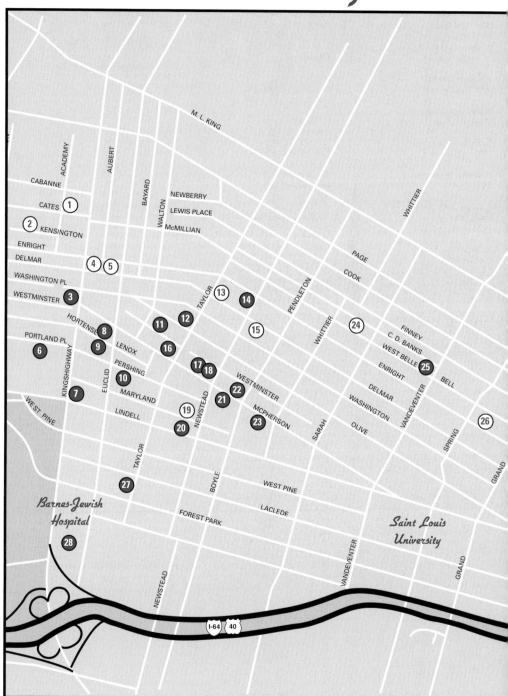

M. L. KING

ACADEMY

AUBERT

CABANNE

BAYARD

NEWBERRY

CATES (1)

WALTON

LEWIS PLACE

WHITTIER

(2) KENSINGTON

McMILLIAN

ENRIGHT

DELMAR

PAGE

WASHINGTON PL

COOK

WESTMINSTER (3)

(4)(5)

TAYLOR

(13)

(14)

PENDLETON

HORTENSE

(8)

(11)

(12)

WHITTIER

(24)

FINNEY

C. D. BANKS

PORTLAND PL

(9)

LENOX

(15)

WEST BELLE

(6)

KINGSHIGHWAY

(16)

ENRIGHT

(25)

BELL

EUCLID

PERSHING

(17)

WESTMINSTER

DELMAR

(10)

(18)

VANDEVENTER

(7)

MARYLAND

(22)

WASHINGTON

(21)

SARAH

WEST PINE

LINDELL

(19)

NEWSTEAD

MCPHERSON

(23)

OLIVE

(20)

SPRING

(26)

TAYLOR

GRAND

(27)

BOYLE

WEST PINE

Barnes-Jewish

LACLEDE

Hospital

FOREST PARK

Saint Louis

University

(28)

VANDEVENTER

GRAND

NEWSTEAD

I-64 40

1. Wolfe, Thomas
5095 Cates Ave.

2. *Meet Me in St. Louis*
5135 Kensington Ave.

3. Barkley, Alben
Washington and Kingshighway Blvds.

4. Hotchner, A. E.
Delmar and Kingshighway Blvds.

5. Williams, Tennessee
4931–4933 Delmar Blvd.

6. Davis, Dwight
16 Portland Pl.

7. Caray, Harry; Prince, Bob
Chase Park Plaza
212 N. Kingshighway Blvd.

8. Lindbergh, Charles
1 Hortense Pl.

9. Walker, David Davis
10 Hortense Pl.

10. Burroughs, William S.
4664 Pershing Ave.

11. Williams, Tennessee
4633 Westminster Pl.

12. Liston, Sonny
4525 Olive St.

13. Davis, Miles
4460 Delmar Blvd.

14. Foxx, Redd
4400 Enright Ave.

15. Berry, Chuck
4352 Delmar Blvd.

16. Moorehead, Agnes
4531 McPherson Ave.

17. Clifford, Clark
4450 Westminster Pl.

18. Eliot, T. S.
4446 Westminster Pl.

19. Francis, David R.
4421 Maryland Ave.

20. Cathedral Basilica
4431 Lindell Blvd.

21. Gellhorn, Martha
4366 McPherson Ave.

22. McLuhan, Marshall
4343 McPherson Ave.

23. Chopin, Kate
4232 McPherson Ave.

24. Armstrong, Henry
4145 W. Belle Pl.

25. Davis, Billy, Jr.
3919 W. Belle Pl.

26. Walker, David Davis
VA Hospital
Between Grand Blvd. and Spring Ave.

27. Williams, Tennessee
5 S. Taylor Ave.

28. Turner, Tina; Williams, Tennessee
Barnes-Jewish Hospital
216 S. Kingshighway Blvd.

Map F: *Clayton, University City*

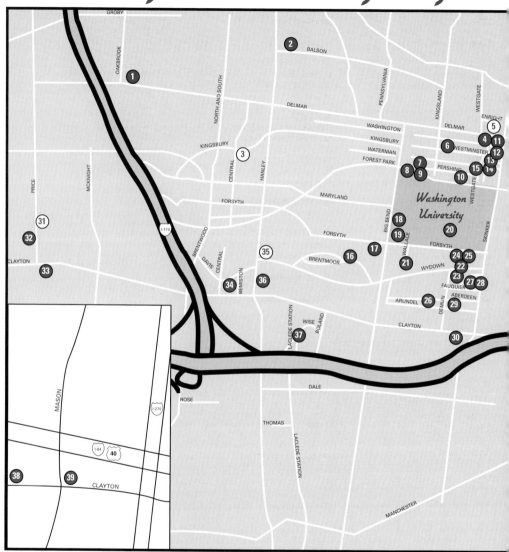

1. **Buchanan, Pat**
8333 Delmar Blvd.

2. **Nelly; Williams, Tennessee**
University City High School
7401 Balson Ave.

3. **Burroughs, William S.**
222 N. Central Ave.

4. **Nelly**
Tivoli Theatre
6350 Delmar Blvd.

5. **Williams, Tennessee**
6254 Enright Ave.

6. **Clifford, Clark**
6633 Kingsbury Pl.

7. **Hartford, John**
6940 Waterman Blvd.

8. **Skouras, Spyros**
6950 Pershing Ave.

9. **Dooley, Tom**
6940 Pershing Ave.

10. **Williams, Tennessee**
6634 Pershing Ave.

11. **Doolittle, Gen. James H.**
6311 Washington Ave.

12. **Gibson, Bob**
6316 Westminster Blvd.

13. **Mead, Shepherd**
6313 Waterman Blvd.

14. **Dooley, Tom**
6314 Waterman Blvd.

15. **Guggenheim, Charles**
329 Westgate Ave.

16. **Danforth, John**
17 Brentmoor Park

17. **Ramis, Harold**
Zeta Beta Tau fraternity house
7020 Forsyth Blvd.

18. **Presidential debates**
Washington University Athletic Center
Forsyth and Big Bend Blvds.

19. **Francis Field; Poage, George**
NE corner of Big Bend and Forsyth Blvds.

20. **U2**
Graham Chapel at Washington University
1 Brookings Dr.

21. **Brookings, Robert S.;**
Compton, Arthur Holly
6510 Wallace Dr.

22. **Williams, Rose**
Church of St. Michael and St. George
6345 Wydown Blvd.

23. **Williams, Tennessee**
6360 Wydown Blvd.

24. **Lewis, A. H.**
6352 Wydown Blvd.

25. **Price, Vincent**
6320 Forsyth Blvd.

26. **Williams, Tennessee**
53 Arundel Pl.

27. **Eagleton, Thomas F.**
268 Woodbourne Dr.

28. **Merrick, David**
MHS Library and Research Center
225 S. Skinker Blvd.

29. **Williams, Tennessee**
42 Aberdeen Pl.

30. ***White Palace***
6300 Clayton Rd.

31. **Burroughs, William S.**
700 Price Rd.

32. **Burroughs, William S.**
John Burroughs School
755 S. Price Rd.

33. **Caray, Harry**
9160 Clayton Rd.

34. **Kline, Kevin**
7800 Davis Dr.

35. **Woods, Tiger**
Near Hanley Rd. and Wydown Blvd.

36. **McGwire, Mark**
750 S. Hanley Rd.

37. **Ashe, Arthur**
1221 Laclede Station Rd.

38. **Phillips, Stone**
Parkway West High School
14563 Clayton Rd.

39. **Duvall, Robert**
The Principia Upper School
13201 Clayton Rd.

Map G: *North City, The Ville*

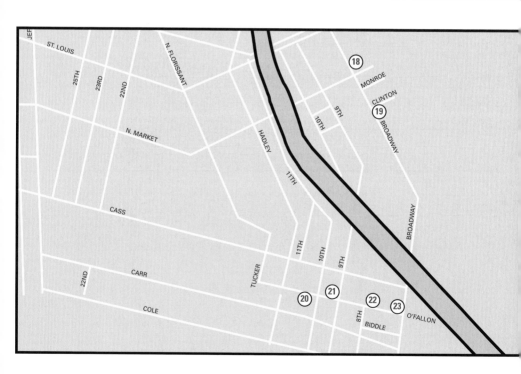

1. Liston, Sonny
4439 Farlin Ave.

2. Shelley, J. D.
4600 Labadie Ave.

3. Gregory, Dick
Cote Brilliante Elementary School
2616 Cora Ave.

4. Liston, Sonny
4454 St. Louis Ave.

5. Berry, Chuck
4319 Labadie Ave.

6. Gregory, Dick
1803 N. Taylor Ave.

7. Berry, Chuck
4420 Cottage Ave.

8. Gregory, Dick; McFerrin, Robert, Sr.
Sumner High School
4248 Cottage Ave.

9. Winters, Shelley
1324 N. Newstead Ave.

10. Bumbry, Grace
1703 Annie Malone Dr.

11. Berry, Chuck
2520 Annie Malone Dr.

12. Berry, Chuck
2742 N. Vandeventer Ave.

**13. Beaumont High School;
Weaver, Earl; Young, Cy**
3836 Natural Bridge Rd.

14. Musial, Stan
3644 Natural Bridge Rd.

15. Merrick, David
3616 N. Garrison St.

**16. Aaron, Hank; Gaedel, Eddie;
Reagan, Ronald; Weaver, Earl**
2901 N. Grand Ave.

17. Armstrong, Henry
2912 St. Louis Ave.

18. Eads, James B.
2300 N. Broadway

19. Eads, James B.
N. Broadway and Clinton St.

20. Liston, Sonny
1006 O'Fallon St.

21. Liston, Sonny
901 O'Fallon St.

22. Carroll, Mickey
8th and O'Fallon Sts.

23. Liston, Sonny
O'Fallon St. and Broadway

Map H: *North County*

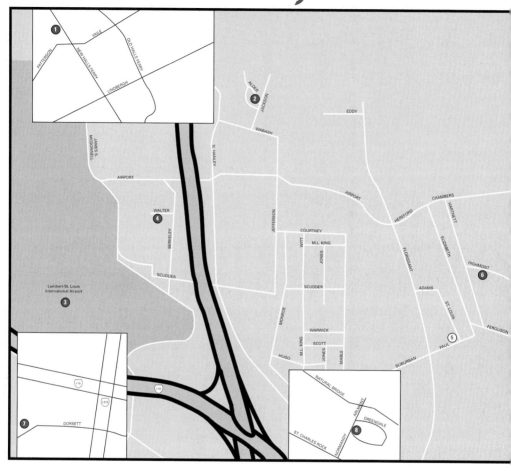

1. Capshaw, Kate
Hazelwood Central High School
15875 New Halls Ferry Rd.

2. Cedric the Entertainer
8422 Alder Ave.

3. *Planes, Trains and Automobiles*
Lambert-St. Louis International Airport

4. Cedric the Entertainer
Berkeley High School
8710 Walter Ave.

5. First monster truck
St. Louis Ave. and Paul Dr.

6. McDonald, Michael
946 Highmont Dr.

7. Peck, Gregory
Creve Coeur Park
2143 Creve Coeur Mill Rd.

8. Thomas, Clarence
1 Greendale Dr.

Map I: *Webster Groves, Affton*

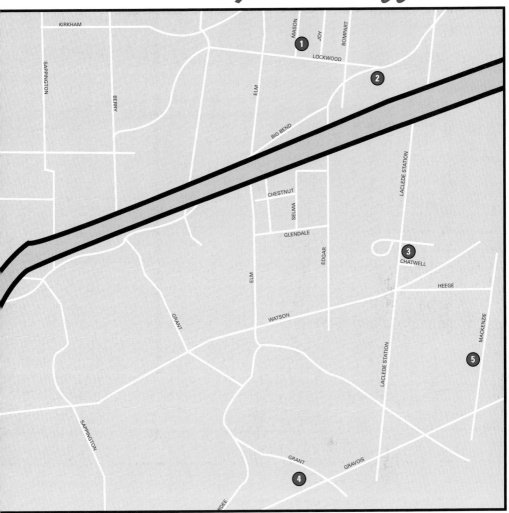

1. Diller, Phyllis
30 Mason Ave.

2. Frann, Mary; Mason, Marsha
Nerinx Hall
530 E. Lockwood Ave.

3. Costas, Bob; Crow, Sheryl
Georgetown Apartments
7880 Chatwell Dr.

4. Grant, Ulysses S.; Kennedy, John F.
Grant's Farm
10501 Gravois Rd.

5. Goodman, John
Affton High School
8309 Mackenzie Rd.

Map J: *South City part 1*

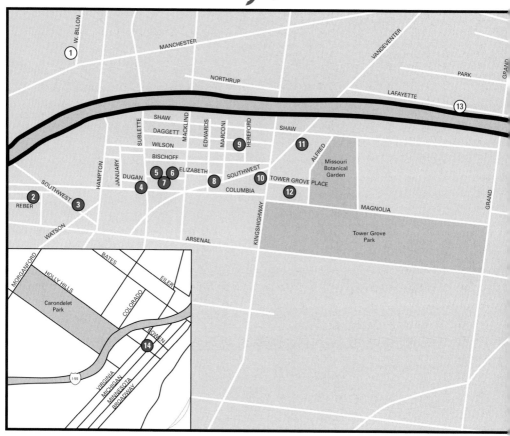

1. *White Palace*
1521 W. Billon Ave.

2. Gephardt, Richard
6263 Reber Pl.

3. Gephardt, Richard
Mason School
6031 Southwest Ave.

4. Berra, Yogi
Joe Fassi Sausage and Sandwich Factory
2325 Sublette Ave.

5. Berra, Yogi
5447 Elizabeth Ave.

6. Buck, Jack
5405 Elizabeth Ave.

7. Garagiola, Joe
5446 Elizabeth Ave.

8. Berra, Yogi
2300 Edwards Ave.

9. Berra, Yogi
St. Ambrose Church
5130 Wilson Ave.

10. Berra, Yogi
Southwest Ave. and Kingshighway Blvd.

11. Berra, Yogi
Wade Grammar School
2030 S. Vandeventer Ave.

12. Eagleton, Thomas F.
4608 Tower Grove Pl.

13. Grable, Betty
3858 Lafayette Ave.

14. Blow, Susan
6303 Michigan Ave.

Map K: *South City part 2*

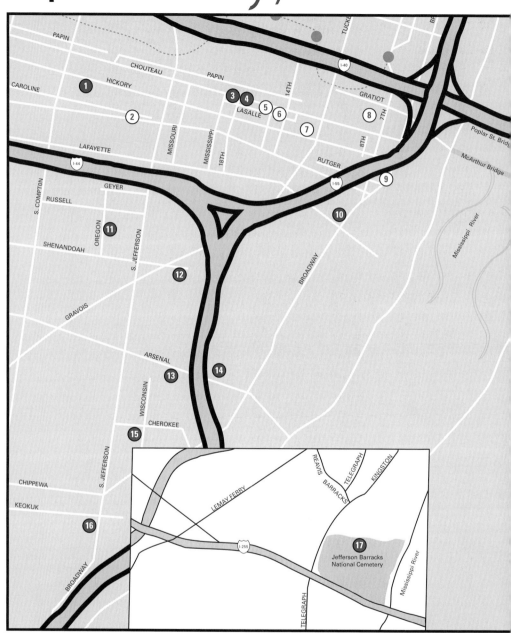

1. Angelou, Maya
3130 Hickory St.

2. Angelou, Maya
2714 ½ Caroline St.

3. Caray, Harry
1909 LaSalle St.

4. Caray, Harry
18th St. and Chouteau Ave.

5. Chopin, Kate
1125 St. Ange Ave.; 1122 St. Ange Ave.

6. Chopin, Kate
1118 St. Ange Ave.

7. Spinks, Leon and Michael
1241 Hickory St.

8. Chopin, Kate
8th St. between Chouteau and Gratiot

9. White, Jo Jo
2 Rutger St.

10. Baker, Josephine
Soulard Market
7th St. and Lafayette Ave.

11. Young, Chic
2148 Oregon Ave.

12. Caray, Harry
1920 Shenandoah Ave.

13. Ray, John
1982 Arsenal St.

14. Chirac, Jacques
Anheuser-Busch Brewery
12th and Lynch Sts.

15. Murray, Bill
2022 Cherokee St.

16. Exorcism
Alexian Brothers Hospital
Broadway and Keokuk St.

**17. Davis, Jefferson;
Eisenhower, Dwight D.;
Grant, Ulysses S.;
Lee, Robert E.;
Sherman, William Tecumseh;
Taylor, Zachary; Twain, Mark**
Jefferson Barracks
533 Grant Rd.

Entries by Subject

Art and Architecture

Cathedral Basilica
Eads, James B.
French, Daniel Chester
Gilbert, Cass
Johnson, Philip
Mullett, A. B.
Planter's Hotel
Sincoff, Jerry
Smith, Luther Ely
Wainwright Building
Young, Chic

Business

Danforth, William H.
D'Arcy, William Cheever
Edwards, Benjamin F.
First gas station
First monster truck
Heron, M. W.
Lewis, A. H.
Martin, William McChesney, Jr. and Sr.
Pulitzer, Joseph
Ray, John
TUMS Building
Walker, David Davis

Education

Beaumont High School
Blow, Susan
Brookings, Robert S.
Compton, Arthur Holly
Inge, William
McLuhan, Marshall
Missouri School for the Blind
Smith, Huston
Soldan High School

Exploration

Charbonneau, Jean Baptiste
Clark, William
Lindbergh, Charles

Film and Television

Angelou, Maya
Baker, Josephine
Bowdern, Father William
Buck, Joe
Capshaw, Kate
Caray, Harry
Carroll, Mickey
Cedric the Entertainer
Costas, Bob
Diller, Phyllis
Duvall, Robert

Escape from New York
Exorcism
Foxx, Redd
Frann, Mary
Goodman, John
Grable, Betty
Gregory, Dick
Guggenheim, Charles
Guillaume, Robert
Hurt, William
Inge, William
Kann, Stan
Kline, Kevin
Mason, Marsha
Meet Me in St. Louis
Moorehead, Agnes
Murray, Bill
National Lampoon's Vacation
Nelly
Peck, Gregory
Philbin, Regis
Phillips, Stone
Planes, Trains and Automobiles
Price, Vincent
Ramis, Harold
Reagan, Ronald
Skouras, Spyros
White Palace
Winters, Shelley

Law

Blackmun, Harry

Brandeis, Louis
Minor, Virginia Louisa
Scott, Dred
Scott, Harriet
Shelley, J. D.
Shenker, Morris
Thomas, Clarence

Literature and Journalism

Angelou, Maya
Burroughs, William S.
Chopin, Kate
Dickens, Charles
Dreiser, Theodore
Eliot, T. S.
Field, Eugene
Gellhorn, Martha
Hotchner, A. E.
Inge, William
Keckly, Elizabeth
McLuhan, Marshall
Mead, Shepherd
Pulitzer, Joseph
Rombauer, Irma
Shange, Ntozake
Smith, Huston
Twain, Mark
White Palace
Whitman, Walt
Williams, Tennessee
Wolfe, Thomas

Military

American Legion
Clark, William
Davis, Jefferson
Doolittle, General James H.
Eisenhower, Dwight D.
Fort San Carlos
Grant, Ulysses S.
Lee, Robert E.
Lyon, Nathaniel
Pontiac
Sherman, William Tecumseh
Taylor, Zachary

Music

Berry, Chuck
Bumbry, Grace
Crow, Sheryl
Davis, Billy, Jr.
Davis, Miles
"Frankie and Johnny"
Handy, W. C.
Hartford, John
Joplin, Scott
McDonald, Michael
McFerrin, Robert, Sr.
Nelly
Stagger Lee
Turner, Tina
U2

Politics

Barkley, Alben
Benton, Thomas Hart
Bradley, Bill
Buchanan, Pat
Chirac, Jacques
Clifford, Clark
Danforth, John
Davis, Dwight
Davis, Jefferson
Eagleton, Thomas F.
Eisenhower, Dwight D.
Francis, David R.
Gephardt, Richard
Grant, Ulysses S.
Kennedy, John F.
Presidential debates
Reagan, Ronald
Revels, Reverend Hiram R.
Roosevelt, Franklin D.
Taylor, Zachary
Tilden, Samuel
Truman, Harry S.

Radio and Broadcasting

Buck, Jack
Buck, Joe
Caray, Harry
Costas, Bob
Dierdorf, Dan
Garagiola, Joe
Prince, Bob

Religion

Bowdern, Father William
Cathedral Basilica
Exorcism
Pope John Paul II
Revels, Rev. Hiram R.
Smith, Huston

Science and Medicine

Compton, Arthur Holly
Dooley, Tom

Sports

Aaron, Hank
Armstrong, Henry
Ashe, Arthur
Beaumont High School
Bell, James "Cool Papa"
Berra, Yogi
Boston Red Sox
Bradley, Bill
Brock, Lou
Buck, Jack
Buck, Joe
Caray, Harry
Connors, Jimmy
Costas, Bob
Davis, Dwight
Dierdorf, Dan
First monster truck
Francis Field

Gaedel, Eddie
Garagiola, Joe
Gibson, Bob
Hornsby, Rogers
Liston, Sonny
McGwire, Mark
Musial, Stan
Poage, George
Prince, Bob
Rickey, Branch
Spinks, Leon and Michael
Stars Park
Weaver, Earl
White, Jo Jo
Woods, Tiger
World Series roommates
Young, Cy

Stage

Baker, Josephine
Bumbry, Grace
Kline, Kevin
McFerrin, Robert, Sr.
Merrick, David
Rockettes

Sources

[g]The books in the column below are referenced frequently and will be referred to only by the last name of the author:

Brennan, Charles, and Ben Cannon. *Walking Historic Downtown St. Louis: 250 Incredible Years in Two Hours or Less!* St. Louis: Virginia Publishing, 2000.

Broeg, Bob. *The 100 Greatest Moments in St. Louis Sports.* St. Louis: Missouri Historical Society Press, 2000.

Cuoco, Lorin, and William H. Gass, eds. *Literary St. Louis: A Guide.* St. Louis: Missouri Historical Society Press, 2000.

Dillon, Dan. *So, Where'd You Go to High School? The Baby Boomer Edition.* St. Louis: Virginia Publishing, 2005.

Gass, Mary Henderson, Jean Fahey Eberle, and Judith Phelps Little. *Parkview: A Saint Louis Urban Oasis, 1905–2005.* St. Louis: Virginia Publishing, 2005.

Savage, Charles C. *Architecture of the Private Streets of St. Louis.* Columbia: University of Missouri Press, 1987.

St. Louis Walk of Fame: 75 Great St. Louisans. St. Louis: St. Louis Walk of Fame, 1998.

Weaver, Earl, with Berry Stainback. *It's What You Learn After You Know It All That Counts.* Garden City, NJ: Doubleday and Co., 1982.

Wright, John A. *Discovering African American St. Louis.* 2nd ed. St. Louis: Missouri Historical Society Press, 2002.

Aaron, Hank
Aaron, Hank. *I Had a Hammer: The Hank Aaron Story.* New York: HarperTorch, 1992.
Heidenry, John, and Brett Topel. *The Boys Who Were Left Behind: The 1944 World Series between the Hapless St. Louis Browns and the Legendary St. Louis Cardinals.* Lincoln: University of Nebraska Press, 2006, 152.

American Legion
"Significant Dates in American Legion History." American Legion.
http://www.legion.org/?section=our_legion &subsection=ol_history&content=ol_ history_1919.

Angelou, Maya
Angelou, Maya. *I Know Why the Caged Bird Sings.* New York: Random House, 1969.
Bloom, Howard, ed. *Modern Critical Views: Maya Angelou.* Philadelphia: Chelsea House, 1998, 219.

Armstrong, Henry
Broeg.
Wright, 50–51.

Ashe, Arthur
Ashe, Arthur, and Arnold Rampersad. *Days of Grace: A Memoir.* New York: Ballantine Books, 1993.
Cobb, Ron. "Arthur Ashe: The Champion Next Door." *St. Louis Post-Dispatch,* July 7, 1982, p. E1.
Learman, Mark. "Black History: Arthur Ashe." *St. Louis Post-Dispatch,* February 27, 2006, p. C1.
Timmerman, Tom. "The Cradle of Tennis." *St. Louis Post-Dispatch,* January 13, 2004.

Baker, Josephine
Smith, JoAnn Adams. *Selected Neighbors and Neighborhoods of North St. Louis and Selected Related Events*. St. Louis: Friends of Vaughn Cultural Center, 1988. *St. Louis Walk of Fame*. Wright, 23–24.

Barkley, Alben
"Barkley-Hadley Wedding Draws Cheers of Crowd." *St. Louis Post-Dispatch*, November 18, 1949, p. 1.
Clifford, Clark, with Richard Holbrooke. *Counsel to the President: A Memoir*. New York: Random House, 1991, 256.

Beaumont High School
Weaver, 81.

Bell, James "Cool Papa"
"Baseball's Cool Papa Bell Dies." *St. Louis Post-Dispatch*, March 8, 1991, p. A1.
Broeg, 76.

Benton, Thomas Hart
Brennan and Cannon.

Berra, Yogi
Berra, Yogi, with Dave Kaplan. *Ten Rings: My Championship Seasons*. New York: William Morrrow, 2003.
Berra, Yogi, with David Kaplan. *When You Come to a Fork in the Road, Take It!* New York: Hyperion, 2001, 83, 104, 108, 125.
Berra, Yogi, with Tom Horton. *Yogi: It Ain't Over*. New York: McGraw-Hill, 1989.

Berry, Chuck
Collis, John. *Chuck Berry: The Biography*. London: Aurum, 2002, 33.
Wright.

Blackmun, Harry
Brennan and Cannon.

Blow, Susan
Cuoco and Gass.
Harris, NiNi, author of *A History of Carondelet* (St. Louis: Patrice Press, 1991), personal interview, July 2005.

Boston Red Sox
Dressel, Charlie, owner of Mount Pleasant Winery in 2003, personal interview, October 2004.
Shaughnessy, Dan, *Boston Globe* reporter, personal interview, June 2005.

Bowdern, Father William
Kraus, Leonard, pastor of St. Francis Xavier College Church, personal interview, June 13, 2006.

Bradley, Bill
Brennan and Cannon.

Brandeis, Louis
Brennan and Cannon.

Brookings, Robert S.
O'Connor, Candace. *Beginning a Great Work: Washington University in St. Louis, 1853–2003*. St. Louis: Washington University in St. Louis, 2003, 79.
Savage, 16, 55–56, 138.

Buchanan, Pat
Buchanan, Pat, personal interview, July 2005.

Buck, Jack
Buck, Jack, Rob Rains, and Bob Broeg. *Jack Buck: "That's a Winner."* Champaign, IL: Sagamore, 1997, 185.
Munz, Michele. "A Place for Fame." *St. Louis Post-Dispatch*, June 2, 2003.

Buck, Joe
Buck, Joe, email message to author, July 3, 2006.

Bumbry, Grace
Wright.

Burroughs, William S.
Cuoco and Gass.

Capshaw, Kate
Dillon, 160–161.

Caray, Harry
Caray, Harry, with Bob Verdi. *Holy Cow!* New York: Villard Books, 1989, 18, 26, 28, 31, 32, 40, 62–63, 162–163.
St. Louis Walk of Fame.

Carroll, Mickey
Copeland, Jeff. "The Wizard's Coroner." *West County Citizen*, April 22, 1981, sec. A, pp. 1, 13.
Rice, Patricia. "Mickey Carroll Will Really, Most Sincerely Celebrate 86th Birthday." *St. Louis Post-Dispatch*, June 30, 2005, sec. S, p. 3.

Cathedral Basilica
Richardson, Ann, and Maureen Kaminski, Cathedral historians, personal interview, May 11, 2006.
Stiritz, Mary M. *St. Louis: Historic Churches and Synagogues.* St. Louis: Landmarks Association of St. Louis, 1995, 96.

Cedric the Entertainer
"Cedric the Entertainer." *2004 Current Biography Yearbook.* New York: H. W. Wilson, 2004, 59–61.
Dillon, 14–15.
Kyles, Rosetta, personal interview, June 10, 2006.

Charbonneau, Jean Baptiste
Brennan and Cannon.

Chirac, Jacques
Chirac, Jacques. Interview with James Graff and Bruce Crumley. *Time*, February 24, 2003, 32–33.

Chopin, Kate
Cuoco and Gass, 154.
Toth, Emily. *Unveiling Kate Chopin.* Jackson: University Press of Mississippi, 1999.

Clark, William
Brennan and Cannon.
Hyde, William, and Howard L. Conard, eds. *Encyclopedia of the History of St. Louis.*

Vol. 1. St. Louis: The Southern History Company, 1899.

Clifford, Clark
Clifford, Clark, with Richard C. Holbrooke. *Counsel to the President: A Memoir.* New York: Random House, 1991.
Sawyer, Jon. "Clark Clifford: Truth Teller Abused, at End, by Lies." *St. Louis Post-Dispatch*, October 15, 1998, p. B7.

Compton, Arthur Holly
Garraty, John A., and Mark C. Carnes, eds. *American National Biography.* Vol. 5. New York: Oxford University Press, 1999.

Connors, Jimmy
McGuire, John M. "Star Power: St. Louis Walk of Fame." *St. Louis Post-Dispatch*, May 1, 2001, p. E1.

Costas, Bob
Davis, Pam, assistant to Costas, personal interview, July 2005.

Crow, Sheryl
Kurrie, Gina, friend of Crow, personal interview, March 30, 2006.

Danforth, John
Fitz, Martha, assistant to Senator Danforth, personal interview, July 2005.

Danforth, William H
Danforth, John, grandson of William Danforth, personal interview, March 29, 2006.
Leonard, John W., ed. *The Book of St. Louisans.* St. Louis: The St. Louis Republic, 1906.

D'Arcy, William Cheever
Brennan and Cannon.

Davis, Billy, Jr
Davis, Billy, Jr., interview on *The Charlie Brennan Show*, KMOX–St. Louis, April 20, 2006.

Davis, Dwight
Byrne, Mrs. John T., 16 Portland Place, personal interview, March 13, 2006.
Christensen, Lawrence O., et al. *Dictionary of Missouri Biography*. Columbia: University of Missouri Press, 1999, 233.
Savage.
St. Louis Walk of Fame.

Davis, Jefferson
Bowman, James C. "Headquarters for Winning the West." *St. Louis Post-Dispatch,* February 29, 1964.

Davis, Miles
Davis, Miles, with Quincy Troupe. *Miles: The Autobiography*. New York: Simon and Schuster, 1989.

Dickens, Charles
Dickens, Charles. *American Notes Etc.* London: Thomas Nelson and Sons, 1842, 187.

Dierdorf, Dan
CBS Sports. "CBS Sports Team." 1995–2006. http://cbs.sportsline.com/cbssports/team/ddierdorf.

Diller, Phyllis
Diller, Phyllis, with Richard Buskin. *Like a Lampshade in a Whorehouse: My Life in Comedy*. New York: J. P. Tarcher/Penguin, 2005, 158.
Morris, Ann. *A Walk in the Park Historic Walking Tour*. Webster Groves, MO: Webster Groves Historical Society, 2002.

Dooley, Tom
Fischer, James T. *Dr. America: The Lives of Thomas A. Dooley, 1927–1961*. Amherst: University of Massachusetts Press, 1997.
Gass, Eberle, and Little, 167.
Glazier, Michael, ed. *The Encyclopedia of the Irish in America*. Notre Dame, IN: University of Notre Dame Press, 1999, 223.

Doolittle, General James H.
Gass, Eberle, and Little, 167.

Dreiser, Theodore
Associates of St. Louis University Libraries. *Literary St. Louis: Noted Authors and St. Louis Landmarks Associated with Them*. St. Louis: The Associates, 1969.

Duvall, Robert
Dillon, 166–167.

Eads, James B.
Dorsey, Florence L. *Road to the Sea: The Story of James B. Eads and the Mississippi River*. New York: Rinehart, 1947, 26.

Eagleton, Thomas F.
Eagleton, Mrs. Thomas (Barbara), personal interview, March 29, 2006.
St. Louis Walk of Fame.

Edwards, Benjamin F.
Savage, 104.

Eisenhower, Dwight D.
Bowman, James C. "Headquarters for Winning the West." *St. Louis Post-Dispatch*, February 29, 1964.
Fusco, Tony. *A Pictorial History of Jefferson Barracks*. St. Louis: n.p., 1969, 12.

Eliot, T. S.
Associates of St. Louis University Libraries. *Literary St. Louis: Noted Authors and St. Louis Landmarks Associated with Them*. St. Louis: The Associates, 1969.
Childs, Marquis W. "Letter Cites City Influence on T. S. Eliot." *St. Louis Post-Dispatch*, February 16, 1964.
Cuoco and Gass.
Post-Dispatch Magazine. July 17, 1994, 12.

Escape from New York
Barbeau, Adrienne. *There Are Worse Things I Could Do*. New York: Carroll and Graf, 2006, 187.

Exorcism
Lampe, Pat, employee in Physicans' Services Department, St. Alexius Hospital, personal interview, July 10, 2006.

Field, Eugene
Brennan and Cannon.
McNulty, Elizabeth. *St. Louis Then and Now*. San Diego: Thunder Bay Press, 2000.

First gas station
Daniel, Jeff. "Fill 'Er Up!... With Some Hi-Test History of the Gas Pump." *St. Louis Post-Dispatch*, August 3, 2005, p. E1.
McGuire, John M. "Made in St. Louis." *St. Louis Post-Dispatch*, November 21, 1999, p. C11.

First monster truck
Bigfoot 30 Years: The Original Monster Truck. St. Louis: Bigfoot 4×4, Inc., 2004.

Fort San Carlos
Primm, James Neal. *Lion of the Valley: St. Louis, Missouri, 1764–1980*. 3rd ed. St. Louis: Missouri Historical Society Press, 1998, 41–43.

Foxx, Redd
"Redd Foxx." *Current Biography Yearbook*. New York: The H. W. Wilson Company, 1972.
Wright, 40.

Francis, David R.
Barnes, Harper. *Standing on A Volcano: The Life and Times of David Rowland Francis*, St. Louis: Missouri Historical Society Press, 2001, 94, 130.
Brennan and Cannon.
Leonard, John W., ed. *The Book of St. Louisans*. St. Louis: The St. Louis Republic, 1906.
Savage, 142.

"Frankie and Johnny"
Brockgreitens, Mary O. "Frankie and Johnnie Paired in Song but Crossed in Love." *St. Louis Life*, June 1995, p. 12.
Wright, 23.

Frann, Mary
Dillon, 138–139.

Gaedel, Eddie
Broeg.
DeWitt, William O., Jr., interview on *The Charlie Brennan Show*, KMOX–St. Louis, January 17, 2005.

Garagiola, Joe
Munz, Michele. "A Place for Fame." *St. Louis Post-Dispatch*, June 2, 2003.

Gellhorn, Martha
Moorehead, Caroline. *Gellhorn: A Twentieth-Century Life*. New York: Henry Holt and Company, 2003.

Gephardt, Richard
Brennan and Cannon.
Gephardt, Richard, personal interview, March 15, 2006.

Gibson, Bob
Gass, Eberle, and Little, 167.

Gilbert, Cass
Irish, Sharon. *Cass Gilbert, Architect: Modern Traditionalist*. New York: Monacelli Press, 1999.
Toft, Carolyn Hewes, with Lynn Josse. *St. Louis: Landmarks and Historic Districts*. St. Louis: Landmarks Association of St. Louis, 2002, 56.

Glass Menagerie, The
Cuoco and Gass.

Goodman, John
Dillon, 5.

Grable, Betty
Pastos, Spero. *Pin Up: The Tragedy of Betty Grable*. New York: Putnam, 1986, 22.
St. Louis Walk of Fame.

Grant, Ulysses S.
Ambrose, Stephen. *To America*. New York: Simon and Schuster, 2004 (excerpted at http://simonsays.com/content/book.cfm?tab=1&pid=424900&agid=2).

Bowman, James C. "Headquarters for Winning the West." *St. Louis Post-Dispatch*, February 29, 1964.
Brennan and Cannon.
Cuoco and Gass.
Fusco, Tony. *A Pictorial History of Jefferson Barracks*. St. Louis: n.p., 1969, 12.

Gregory, Dick
Gregory, Dick, with Robert Lipsyte. *Nigger: An Autobiography*. New York: Pocket, 1990, 54, 60, 61.
St. Louis Walk of Fame.

Guggenheim, Charles
Gass, Eberle, and Little, 165.

Guillaume, Robert
Guillaume, Robert, with David Ritz. *Guillaume: A Life*. Columbia: University of Missouri Press, 2002, 9, 19, 37.

Handy, W. C.
Brennan and Cannon.
Niese, Jay. "The Music Goes Round and Round." *St. Louis Post-Dispatch*, January 24, 1995, p. D1.

Hartford, John
Hamilton, Esley. *Ames Place: A Brief History of Its Planning and Development*. University City, MO: Historical Society of University City, 1991.

Heron, M. W.
Lee, Thomas. "Local Company Crafts New Ads for Old Liquor: Southern Comfort Puts $16 Million into Effort." *St. Louis Post-Dispatch*, August 20, 2002, p. C1.

Hornsby, Rogers
Prost, Charlene. "Jefferson Arms Hopes to Dust off Its Past." *St. Louis Post-Dispatch*, August 11, 1997, p. 12.

Hotchner, A. E.
Hotchner, A. E. *King of the Hill*. New York: Harper and Row, 1972, 3.

Inge, William
Cuoco and Gass, 203, 205.

Johnson, Philip
McCue, George, and Frank Peters. *A Guide to the Architecture of St. Louis*. Columbia: University of Missouri Press, 1989, 38.

Joplin, Scott
Wright, 34.

Kann, Stan
Delaney, Norman, personal interview, August 3, 2005.

Keckly, Elizabeth
Wright, 13.

Kennedy, John F.
Eagleton, Mrs. Thomas (Barbara), personal interview, June 25, 2006.
O'Neill, Tip, with William Novak. *Man of the House: The Life and Political Memories of Speaker Tip O'Neill*. New York: St. Martin's Press, 1987, 113–114.

Kline, Kevin
Devlin, Albert J., and Nancy M. Tischler, eds. *The Selected Letters of Tennessee Williams*. Vol. 1, 1920–1945. New York: New Directions, 2000, 92.
Polk's St. Louis County (Missouri) Directory. Taylor, MI: R. L. Polk, 1955.

Lee, Robert E.
Bowman, James C. "Headquarters for Winning the West." *St. Louis Post-Dispatch,* February 29, 1964.

Lewis, A. H.
Stohr, Mary Ann. "A Brief History of the Newman House: The Catholic Student Center at Washington University." October 21, 1996. http://www.washucsc.org/v2/house.php.

Lindbergh, Charles
Lindbergh, Charles. *The Spirit of St. Louis*. New York: Scribner, 1953.

Liston, Sonny
Tosches, Nick. *The Devil and Sonny Liston*. Boston: Little, Brown, 2000, 38, 40–42, 56, 63, 93, 98.

Lyon, Nathaniel
Gerteis, Louis S. *Civil War St. Louis*. Lawrence: University Press of Kansas, 2001.

Martin, William McChesney, Jr. and Sr.
Brennan and Cannon.
Peterson, Melody. "William McChesney Martin, 91, Dies; Defined Fed's Role." *New York Times*, July 29, 1998, p. A18.

Mason, Marsha
Dillon, 138–139.

McDonald, Michael
Duncan, Dan, boyhood friend of McDonald, personal interview, July 2005.

McFerrin, Robert, Sr.
Dillon, 226.

McGwire, Mark
Doorman at the Claytonian and local merchants, personal interviews, March 31, 2006.
"Mark McGwire." Baseball Library. 2002. http://www.baseballlibrary.com/base balllibrary/ballplayers/M/McGwire_ Mark.stm

McLuhan, Marshall
Cuoco and Gass, 142.

Mead, Shepherd
Gass, Eberle, and Little, 167.

Meet Me in St. Louis
Cuoco and Gass, 166–168.
Meet Me in St. Louis, directed by Vincente Minnelli (1944; Century City, CA: MGM).

Merrick, David
Dillon, 24–25.
Kissel, Howard. *David Merrick, the Abominable Showman: The Unauthorized Biography*. New York: Applause, 1993, 32, 35, 43, 47.

Minor, Virginia Louisa
Sherr, Lynn, and Jurate Kazickas. *The American Woman's Gazetteer*. New York: Bantam Books, 1976, 133.

Missouri School for the Blind
Sucharski, James, Missouri School for the Blind superintendent, personal interview, July 2005.

Moorehead, Agnes
Tranberg, Charles, author of *I Love the Illusion: The Life and Career of Agnes Moorehead*, personal communication, July 14, 2005.

Mullett, A. B.
Toft, Carolyn Hewes, with Lynn Josse. *St. Louis: Landmarks and Historic Districts*. St. Louis: Landmarks Association of St. Louis, 2002, 35.

Murray, Bill
Larger Than Life, DVD, directed by Howard Franklin (1996; Century City, CA: MGM, 2003).

Musial, Stan
"Fairgrounds Park Place on Historic Register." *News and Views* 11, no. 1 (Winter 2003). http://www.kohner.com/ news_win03.htm.
Lansche, Jerry. *Stan "The Man" Musial: Born to be a Ballplayer*. Dallas: Taylor Publishing, 1994, 20.

National Lampoon's Vacation
Vacation, DVD, directed by Harold Ramis (1983; Burbank, CA: Warner Bros., 2003).

Nelly
Dillon, 232.

Peck, Gregory
Peck, Gregory, interview on *The Charlie Brennan Show*, St. Louis, KMOX–St. Louis, March 22, 1997.

Philbin, Regis
Philbin, Regis, personal interview, December 9, 2005.

Phillips, Stone
Dillon, 160–161.

Planes, Trains and Automobiles
Planes, Trains and Automobiles, DVD,
    directed by John Hughes (1987;
    Hollywood, CA: Paramount, 2002).

Planter's Hotel
Brennan and Cannon.
Dickens, Charles. *American Notes Etc.*
    London: Thomas Nelson and Sons,
    1842, 186.

Poage, George
Wright, 59.

Pontiac
Brennan and Cannon.

Pope John Paul II
Brennan and Cannon.

Presidential debates
Leight, Jasper, Washington University
    spokesperson, personal interview, July
    2005.

Price, Vincent
"Historic Inventory of St. Louis County
    Buildings, The." St. Louis County Parks.
    1994. http://www.co.stlouis.mo.us/
    parks/historical-buildings/Charlack-
    CreveCoeur.html.

Prince, Bob
Buck, Jack, Rob Rains, and Bob Broeg.
    Jack Buck: "That's a Winner."
    Champaign, IL: Sagamore, 1997, 93.

Pulitzer, Joseph
Brennan and Cannon.
Cuoco and Gass.

Ramis, Harold
"Map to ZBT." Zeta Beta Tau.
    http://greeks.wustl.edu/~zbt/map.htm.

Ray, John
Posner, Gerald L. *Killing the Dream: James
    Earl Ray and the Assassination of
    Martin Luther King, Jr.* San Diego:
    Harcourt Brace and Co., 1998, 204.
Report of the Select Committee on
    Assassinations, U.S. House of
    Representatives, Ninety-fifth Congress,
    Second Session: Findings and
    Recommendations. Washington D.C.:
    United States Government Printing
    Office, 1979.

Reagan, Ronald
Caray, Harry. *Holy Cow.* New York: Villard
    Books, 1989, 10.
"Ronald Reagan Calls for Stop to
    'Encroaching Federal Controls.'" *St.
    Louis Commerce*, February 1962, 17.

Revels, Reverend Hiram R.
Wright, 15.

Rickey, Branch
Broeg.
"Rickey, (Wesley) Branch (1881–1965)."
    Biography Channel. 1996–2006.
    http://www.biography.com/search/
    article.do?id=9458118.

Rockettes
Brown, Dennis. "You'd Better Not Pout:
    Pick Your Christmas Present: High-kick-
    ing Revue or Wickedly Funny Memoir."
    The Riverfront Times, December 15,
    2004.
Radio City Music Hall. "The History of the
    Rockettes."
    http://www.radiocity.com/rc_rockette_i
    ndex.html.

Roosevelt, Franklin
St. Louis Globe-Democrat, October 14,
    1936, p. A1.

Scott, Dred
Brennan and Cannon.

Scott, Harriet
Gould's St. Louis Directory for 1875. St.
    Louis: David B. Gould, 1874, 826.
Registry of Deaths, St. Louis (city). Vol. 7.
    Missouri Department of Vital Records,
    131.
Wittenauer, Cheryl. "Researchers Gain
    New Insight into Harriet Scott's Life."
    Kansas City Star, March 7, 2006.

Shange, Ntozake
"Ntozake Shange." ReadMOre. March 30, 2005. http://www.mohumanities.org/ programs/readmore/shange.htm.
St. Louis Post-Dispatch Magazine, July 17, 1994, pp. 12–13.

Shelley, J. D.
Wright, 76–77.

Shenker, Morris
Vittert, Mark, personal interview, July 2005.

Sherman, William Tecumseh
Bowman, James C. "Headquarters for Winning the West." *St. Louis Post-Dispatch*, February 29, 1964.
Sherman, William Tecumseh. *Memoirs of General W. T. Sherman*. New York: The Library of America, 1990, 186.

Sincoff, Jerry
Sincoff, Jerry, personal interview, July 11, 2006.

Skouras, Spyros
Hamilton, Esley. *Ames Place: A Brief History of Its Planning and Development*. St. Louis: Historical Society of University City, 1991, 10.

Smith, Huston
Hodges, Sam. "Rock of Age: For Nearly 50 Years, Huston Smith Has Studied the World's Religions. He's Still at It." *The Dallas Morning News,* October 15, 2005.
Smith, Huston. *Essays on World Religion*. New York: Paragon House, 1992, xxi, xxii.
Nishpapananda, Swami, Vedanta Society of St. Louis, personal interview, June 24, 2006.

Smith, Luther Ely
Moore, Bob, historian, National Park Service, personal interview, March 30, 2006.
St. Louis Post-Dispatch, November 18, 1949.

Soldan High School
McGuire, John M. "Soldan." *St. Louis Post-Dispatch*, March 19, 1982.

Spinks, Leon and Michael
Grossfeld, Stan. "I Can Eat, Breathe, Sleep. I Ain't Gonna Pressurise My Brother for Money." *The Observer*, March 5, 2006.
Wright, 96.

Stagger Lee
Roberts, Randall. "Arch Madness." *The Riverfront Times*, March 30, 2005.

Stars Park
Broeg, 76.
Wright.

Taylor, Zachary
Bowman, James C. "Headquarters for Winning the West." *St. Louis Post-Dispatch,* February 29, 1964.

Thomas, Clarence
"Clarence Thomas." *Current Biography Yearbook 1992.* New York: H. W. Wilson, 1992, 568.
Hunot, Linda, current occupant at 1 Greendale Drive, personal interview, June 24, 2006.

Tilden, Samuel
Brennan and Cannon.

Truman, Harry S.
Brennan and Cannon.
Leroux, Charles. "7 Blunders of Chicago." *Chicago Tribune*, March 9, 2006.

TUMS Building
Brennan and Cannon.

Turner, Tina
Bego, Mark. *Tina Turner: Break Every Rule*. Lanham, MD: Taylor Trade Publishing, 2003, 56.

Twain, Mark
Brennan and Cannon.
Cuoco and Gass, 69.
Mark Twain Centennial, 1835–1935, Hannibal, Missouri. Hannibal, MO: Standard Printing, 1935.
Powers, Ron. *Mark Twain: A Life*. New York: Free Press, 2005, 97.

Richardson, Albert D. *A Personal History of U. S. Grant.* Hartford, CT: American, 1868.

Twain, Mark. *Adventures of Huckleberry Finn.* New York: Charles L. Webster and Company, 1885.
Twain, Mark. *Mississippi Writings.* New York: Viking Press, 1982.

U2
Durchholz, Daniel. "When U2 Played Wash U." *The St. Louis Post-Dispatch,* December 11, 2005, p. F1.

Wainwright Building
Brennan and Cannon.

Walker, David Davis
Savage, 154.

Weaver, Earl
McClellan, Bill. "In Days Gone By, City All-Stars Were 'Resourceful' Types." *St. Louis Post-Dispatch,* July 11, 2001, p. B1.
Weaver, 80, 81, 98.
Weaver, Earl. "Weaver on Strategy." *St. Louis Post-Dispatch,* April 29, 1984.

White, Jo Jo
Mallozzi, Vincent M. *Basketball: The Legends of the Game.* Buffalo, NY: Firefly Books, 1998, 333.
White, Jo Jo, interview on *The Charlie Brennan Show,* KMOX–St. Louis, June 6, 2006.

White Palace
Savan, Glenn. *White Palace.* New York: Bantam, 1987.
White Palace, DVD, directed by Luis Mandoki (1990; Burbank, CA: 2005).

Whitman, Walt
Cuoco and Gass, 21.

Williams, Rose
Devlin, Albert J., and Nancy M. Tischler, eds. *The Selected Letters of Tennessee Williams.* Vol. 1, 1920–1945. New York: New Directions Publishing, 2000, 86.

Williams, Tennessee
Cuoco and Gass, 195–199, 201.
Devlin, Albert J., and Nancy M. Tischler, eds. *The Selected Letters of Tennessee Williams.* Vol. 1, 1920–1945. New York: New Directions Publishing, 2000, 9, 26, 53, 65–66, 81, 135–136, 289, 367.
———, eds. *The Selected Letters of Tennessee Williams.* Vol. 2, 1945–1957. New York: New Directions, 2004, 595.

Winters, Shelly
Winters, Shelley. *Shelley: Also Known as Shirley.* New York: William Morrow & Company, 1980, 16–17.

Wolfe, Thomas
Cuoco and Gass.

Woods, Tiger
Pasco, Jean O. "Woods Puts Homework Before Golf—Again." *Los Angeles Times,* February 11, 2006.
Woods, Tiger. "My Longest Drive." *Golf Digest,* December 2001.

World Series roommates
Heidenry, Jack, and Brett Topel. *The Boys Who Were Left Behind: The 1944 World Series between the Hapless St. Louis Browns and the Legendary St. Louis Cardinals.* Lincoln: University of Nebraska Press, 2006, 16.

Young, Chic
Martin, Dan. "Dagwood and Blondie: St. Louisan's Creation Sandwiches in 75 Years of Wedded Bliss between Naps on the Couch." *St. Louis Post-Dispatch,* Sunday September 4, 2005, p. EV6.

Young, Cy
Broeg, 3.

About the Authors

Charlie Brennan hosts *The Charlie Brennan Show* weekday mornings on KMOX Radio-St. Louis, where he has worked since 1988. He also appears as a regular panelist on KETC-TV's weekly news discussion show *Donnybrook*. The author of *Walking Historic Downtown St. Louis: 250 Incredible Years in Two Hours or Less!* with Ben Cannon, he lives in St. Louis with his wife, Beth Stohr, and their two children.

Bridget Garwitz studies at the Missouri School of Journalism with concentrations in strategic communication and political science. She anchors morning newscasts at KBIA Radio, mid-Missouri's NPR affiliate.

Joe Lattal has broadcast a weekly college music program on WVFI Radio while attending the University of Notre Dame and has hosted NDTV's *Late Night Notre Dame*, a comedy and talk show. He has lived in Chesterfield, Missouri, since 1995.

Acknowledgments

This book was a true collaborative undertaking. The authors are indebted to the many whose publications on St. Louis history preceded this one.

I am thankful to the individuals who not only answered our queries but also took valuable time out of their own schedules to retrieve information. They include June Wuest Becht, Gary Braun, Joe Buck, Pam Davis, Barbara Eagleton, Martha Fitz, Ed Griesedieck, Ruth Ann Abels Hager, Bill Kelly, Gina Kurre, Rosetta Kyles, Dan Martin, John Maurath, John McGuire, and Bob Moore.

I would like to acknowledge Avi Munk, now studying at Yeshivat Sha'alvim in Israel, who provided research assistance. Bridget Garwitz and Joe Lattal supplied the enthusiasm and legwork that got this project off the ground.

I am grateful to Dr. Robert R. Archibald, President, and Victoria W. Monks, Director of Publications, at the Missouri Historical Society for their willingness to take a risk on this unorthodox project.

Big acknowledgments, if not credit on the cover, belong to editors Lauren Mitchell and Keri O'Brien. They tightened, shaped, questioned, double-checked, corrected, recorrected, and rephrased this text. Their love of history, keen eyes, attention to detail, and patience with the authors saved this book from certain doom.

Finally, thanks to my wife Beth, as if she didn't have enough to do, who covered for me at home while I was working on this project. She, with Charlie and Lynly, paid the price for the husband and dad who was off playing author. I love you.

—Charlie Brennan